北京市国民经济主要指标
MAIN NATIONAL ECONOMIC INDICATORS OF BEIJING

人口
Population

年末全市常住人口 2 154.2万人
Permanent Population (year-end)
21.542 million

年末户籍人口 1 375.8万人
Registered Population (year-end)
13.758 million

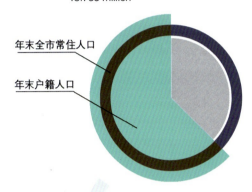

国民经济核算
National Accounts

地区生产总值（GDP）30 320.0亿元
Gross Domestic Product 3 032.00 billion yuan

第一产业 118.7亿元
Primary Industry 11.87 billion yuan

第二产业 5 647.7亿元
Secondary Industry 564.77 billion yuan

第三产业 24 553.6亿元
Tertiary Industry 2 455.36 billion yuan

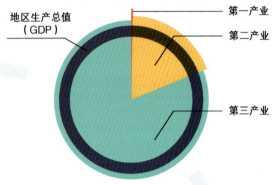

财政
Government Finance

一般公共预算收入 5 785.9亿元
Local Public Budgetary Revenue 578.59 billion yuan

一般公共预算支出 7 471.4亿元
Local Public Budgetary Expenditures 747.14 billion yuan

价格指数（上年=100）
Price Index (Preceding Year = 100)

居民消费价格指数
Consumer Price Index
102.5%

商品零售价格指数
Retail Price Index
101.1%

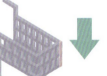

能源消费总量增速 2.6%
Total Energy Consumption Year-on-year Growth Rate 2.6%

全社会固定资产投资增速 -9.9%
Total Investment in Fixed Assets Year-on-year Growth Rate -9.9%

2018年北京市交通运输主要指标
MAIN TRANSPORT INDICATORS OF BEIJING (2018)

综合指标
Comprehensive Index

中心城交通指数5.5
Traffic Index of Core Area 5.5

中心城绿色出行比例73.0%
Green Travel Ratio of Core Area 73.0%

机动车保有量608.4万辆
Number of Motor Vehicles 6.084 million vehicles

交通基础设施
Transport Infrastructure

公路里程22 256公里
Length of Highway 22 256 kms

公路网密度135.62公里/百平方公里
Highway Density 135.62 km/100 sq. km

公共电汽车停车保养场个数677个
Buses and Trolley Buses Parking Lots 677

公交专用道长度952公里
Bus Lane Length 952 km

公路桥梁673 475/6 677米/座
Highway Bridges 673 475/6 677 m/unit

公路隧道102 552/135米/处
Highway Tunnels 102 552/135 m/unit

城市道路里程6 203公里
Length of Urban Roads 6 203 kms

城市桥梁座数2 156座
Number of Urban Bridges 2 156

城市立交桥系个数435个
Number of Urban Overpasses 435

轨道交通运营线路长度636公里
Rail Transit Operation Route Length 636 km

轨道交通车站391个
Rail Transit Station 391 unit

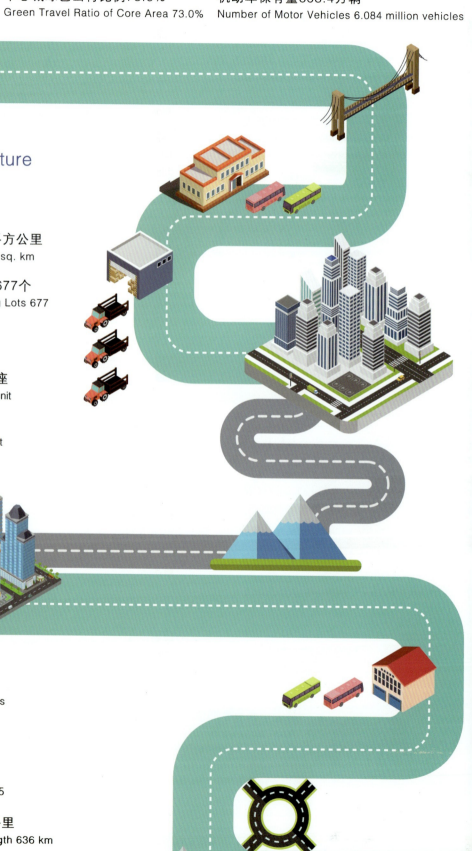

2018年北京市交通运输主要指标
MAIN TRANSPORT INDICATORS OF BEIJING (2018)

客货运输
Passenger and Freight Transportation

载客汽车75 262辆
Passenger Vehicles 75 262

载货汽车168 626辆
Freight Vehicles 168 626

客运量44 175万人次
Passenger Traffic 441.75 million person-times

货运量20 278万吨
Freight Traffic 202.78 million tons

旅客周转量993 699万人公里
Passenger Turnover 9 936.99 million person-kms

货物周转量1 674 068万吨公里
Freight Turnover 16 740.68 million ton-kms

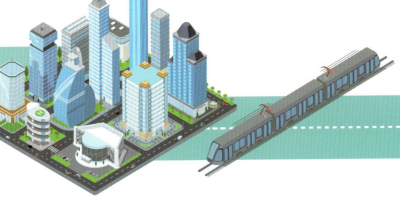

轨道交通客运量384 843万人次
Rail Transit Passenger Volume 3 848.43 million person-times

轨道交通最高日客运量1 349万人次
Maximum Daily Passenger Volume of Rail Transit 13.49 million person-times

公共电汽车客运量318 975万人次
Buses and Trolley Buses Passenger Volume 3189.75 million person-times

公共电汽车最高日客运量1 170万人次
Maximum Daily Passenger Volume of Buses and Trolley Buses 11.70 million person-times

出租汽车客运量34 021万人次
Taxi Passenger Traffic 340.21 million person-times

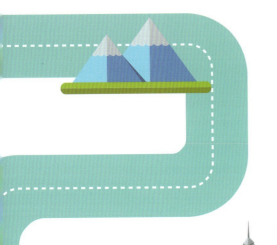
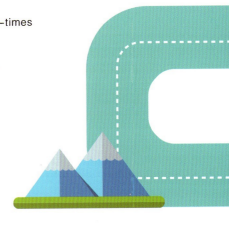

2018年北京市城市道路里程构成图
COMPONENT OF BEIJING URBAN ROAD MILEAGE

城市道路里程构成图
Component of Urban Road Mileage

城市道路 Urban road	里程（公里） Mileage（km）
快速路 Rapid Road	390
主干路 Trunk Road	998
次干路 Secondary Trunk Road	632
支路及以下 Branch road and below	4 183

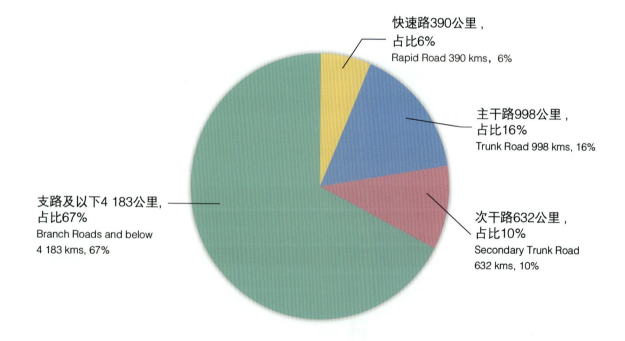

2018年北京市公路里程构成图（按行政等级\技术等级分）
2018 BEIJING HIGHWAY MILEAGE STRUCTURE CHART (BY ADMINISTRATIVE LEVEL\BY TECHNICAL GRADE)

按行政等级分
By Administrative Level

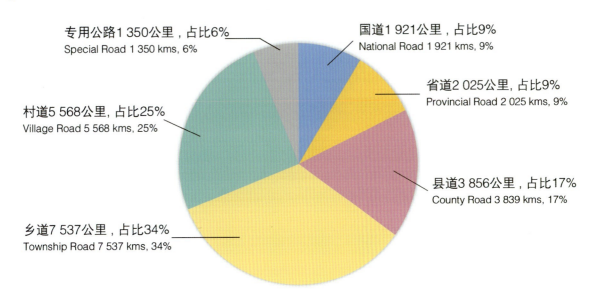

- 专用公路1 350公里，占比6% / Special Road 1 350 kms, 6%
- 国道1 921公里，占比9% / National Road 1 921 kms, 9%
- 省道2 025公里，占比9% / Provincial Road 2 025 kms, 9%
- 县道3 856公里，占比17% / County Road 3 839 kms, 17%
- 乡道7 537公里，占比34% / Township Road 7 537 kms, 34%
- 村道5 568公里，占比25% / Village Road 5 568 kms, 25%

按技术等级分
By Technical Grade

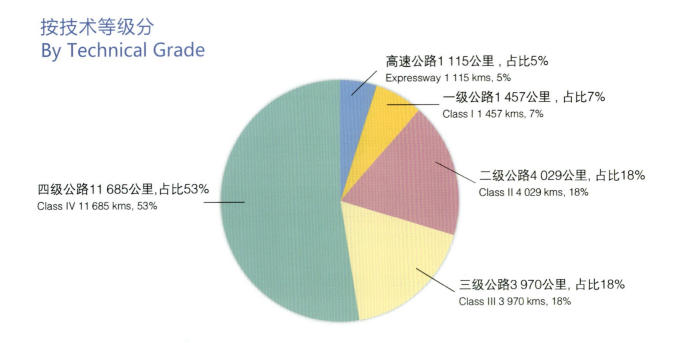

- 高速公路1 115公里，占比5% / Expressway 1 115 kms, 5%
- 一级公路1 457公里，占比7% / Class I 1 457 kms, 7%
- 二级公路4 029公里，占比18% / Class II 4 029 kms, 18%
- 三级公路3 970公里，占比18% / Class III 3 970 kms, 18%
- 四级公路11 685公里，占比53% / Class IV 11 685 kms, 53%

历年北京市公路里程表
LENGTH OF BEIJING HIGHWAY OVER THE YEARS

年度 Year	里程（公里） Mileage（km）
2006	20 503
2007	20 754
2008	20 340
2009	20 755
2010	21 113
2011	21 347
2012	21 492
2013	21 673
2014	21 849
2015	21 885
2016	22 026
2017	22 226
2018	22 256

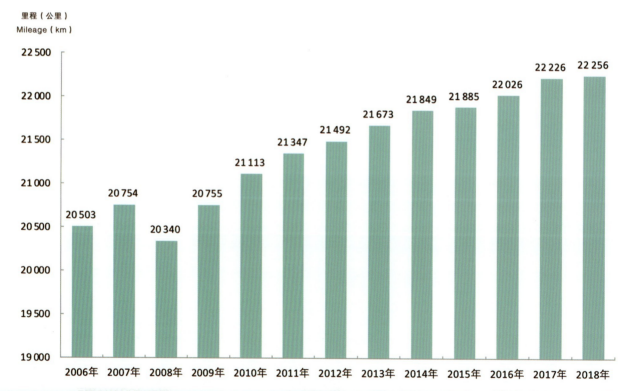

历年北京市高速公路里程
LENGTH OF BEIJING EXPRESSWAY OVER THE YEARS

年度 Year	里程（公里） Mileage（km）
2006	625
2007	628
2008	777
2009	884
2010	903
2011	912
2012	923
2013	923
2014	982
2015	982
2016	1 013
2017	1 013
2018	1 115

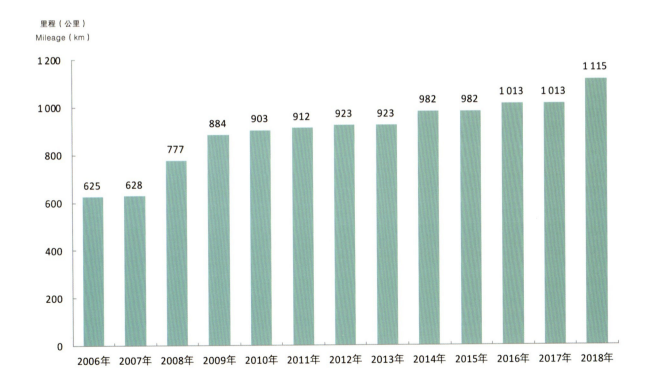

历年北京市城市道路里程
LENGTH OF BEIJING URBAN ROAD OVER THE YEARS

年度 Year	里程（公里）Mileage（km）
2010	6 235
2011	6 258
2012	6 271
2013	6 295
2014	6 426
2015	6 423
2016	6 373
2017	6 359
2018	6 203

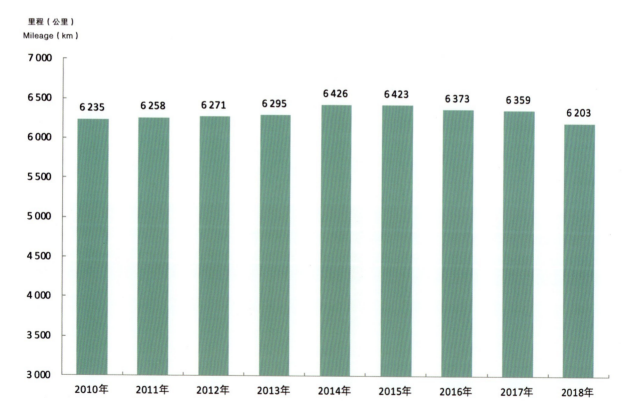

历年北京市轨道交通运营里程
OPERATION LENGTH OF BEIJING RAIL TRANSIT OVER THE YEARS

年度 Year	里程（公里） Mileage（km）
2010	336
2011	372
2012	442
2013	465
2014	527
2015	554
2016	574
2017	608
2018	636

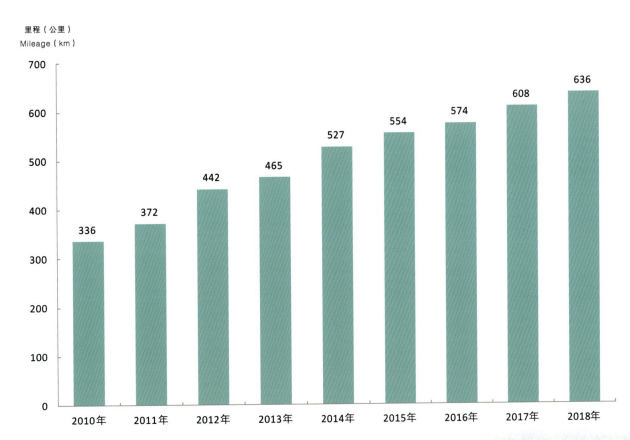

历年北京市公路客运量
Highway Passenger Transportation Volume of Beijing over the Years

年度 Year	公路客运量（万人次） Highway Passenger Transportation Volume of Beijing over the Years（ten thousand person-times）
2013	52 481
2014	52 354
2015	49 931
2016	48 040
2017	44 940
2018	44 175

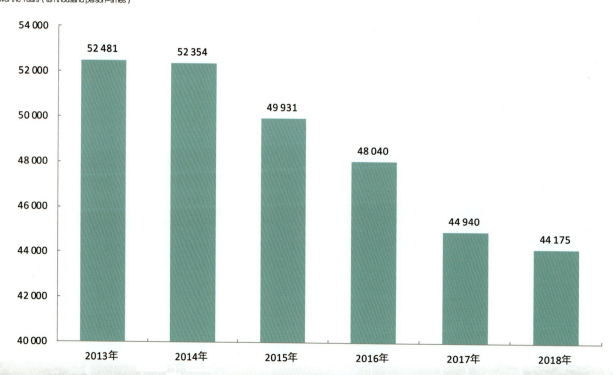

历年北京市公路客运量（万人次）
Highway Passenger Transportation Volume of Beijing over the Years（ten thousand person-times）

历年北京市省际客运站客运量
INTER-PROVINCIAL PASSENGER STATION TRAFFIC OF BEIJING OVER THE YEARS

年度 Year	省际客运站客运量（万人次） Inter-Provincial Passenger Station Traffic (ten thousand person-times)
2006	2 386
2007	2 571
2008	2 530
2009	2 496
2010	2 535
2011	2 742
2012	2 734
2013	2 674
2014	2 669
2015	2 361
2016	1 994
2017	1 771
2018	1 447

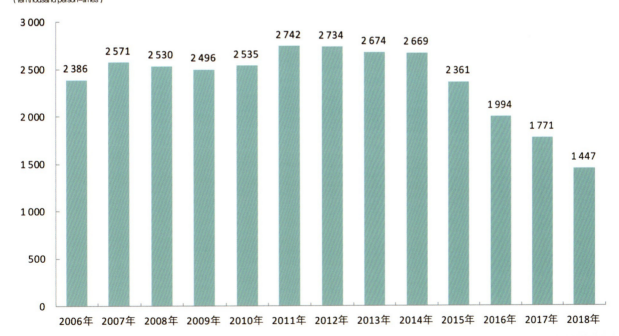

历年公共交通客运量
PUBLIC TRANSPORT PASSENGER TRAFFIC OF BEIJING OVER THE YEARS

年度 Year	公共交通客运量（亿人次） Public Transport Passenger Traffic (100 million person-times)
2006	46.8
2007	48.8
2008	59.3
2009	65.9
2010	69.0
2011	72.3
2012	76.2
2013	80.5
2014	81.6
2015	73.8
2016	73.5
2017	71.3
2018	70.4

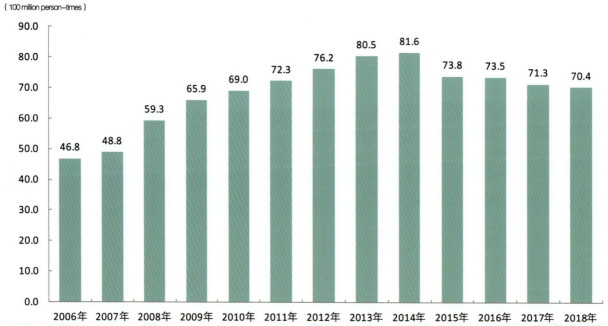

历年北京市公共电汽车客运量
BUSES AND TROLLEY BUSES PASSENGER TRAFFIC OF BEIJING OVER THE YEARS

年度 Year	公共电汽车（亿人次） Buses And Trolley Buses Passenger Traffic （100 million person-times）
2006	39.8
2007	42.3
2008	47.1
2009	51.7
2010	50.5
2011	50.3
2012	51.5
2013	48.4
2014	47.7
2015	40.6
2016	36.9
2017	33.6
2018	31.9

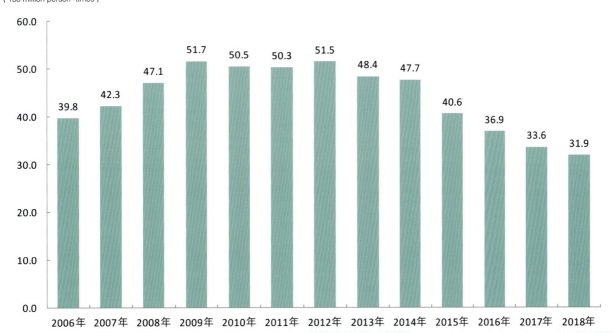

历年北京市轨道交通客运量
RAIL TRANSIT PASSENGER TRAFFIC OF BEIJING OVER THE YEARS

年度 Year	轨道交通（亿人次） Rail Transit Passenger Traffic （100 million person-times）
2006	7.0
2007	6.5
2008	12.2
2009	14.2
2010	18.5
2011	21.9
2012	24.6
2013	32.0
2014	33.9
2015	33.2
2016	36.6
2017	37.8
2018	38.5

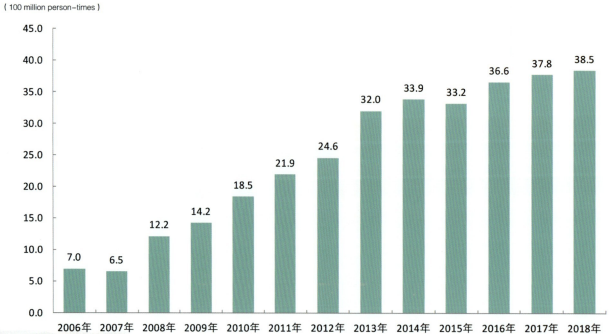

2018年北京市中心城交通出行方式构成图
COMPONENT OF TRANSPORT MODES IN CENTRAL AREA OF BEIJING (2018)

出行方式 Transport Modes	2018年
公共电汽车 Buses And Trolley Buses	16.1%
轨道交通 Rail Transit	16.2%
自行车 Bicycle	11.5%
步行 Walk	29.2%
小汽车 Car	23.3%
出租汽车 Taxi	2.6%
其他 Others	1.1%

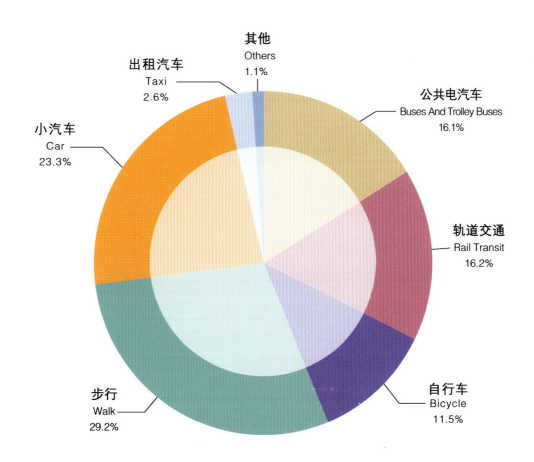

北京交通统计年鉴 2018

北京市交通委员会 编
Beijing Municipal Committee of Transport

人民交通出版社股份有限公司

图书在版编目（CIP）数据

2018北京交通统计年鉴/北京市交通委员会编.
—北京：人民交通出版社股份有限公司，2019.12
ISBN 978-7-114-16094-3

Ⅰ.①2… Ⅱ.①北… Ⅲ.①交通运输业—统计资料—北京—2018—年鉴 Ⅳ.①F512.71-54

中国版本图书馆CIP数据核字（2019）第273552号

书　　名：	2018北京交通统计年鉴
著 作 者：	北京市交通委员会
责任编辑：	陈　鹏
责任校对：	张　贺
出版发行：	人民交通出版社股份有限公司
地　　址：	（100011）北京市朝阳区安定门外外馆斜街3号
网　　址：	http://www.ccpress.com.cn
销售电话：	（010）59757973
总 经 销：	人民交通出版社股份有限公司发行部
经　　销：	各地新华书店
印　　刷：	北京印匠彩色印刷有限公司
开　　本：	880×1230　1/16
印　　张：	8.5
字　　数：	363千
版　　次：	2019年12月　第1版
印　　次：	2019年12月　第1次印刷
书　　号：	ISBN 978-7-114-16094-3
定　　价：	200.00元

（有印刷、装订质量问题的图书由本公司负责调换）

《2018 北京交通统计年鉴》

编委会

主　　　任：李先忠

常务副主任：孙中阁

副 主 任（按姓氏笔画排序）：

　　　　　王兆荣　王春强　方　平　孟　桥　容　军　逯福全

　　　　　边伟芳　冯建民　郭卫亮　商万友　常华民　钟志敏

编　　　委（按姓氏笔画排序）：

　　　　　马　瑞　王　昊　冯　杰　冯　德　曲　峰　刘春杰

　　　　　孙宁宁　孙壮志　李　鑫　吴　洁　张德欣　周　红

　　　　　单　明　秦海涛　高增华　赵　震　刘长革　李亚宁

　　　　　杨宇梁　王众毅　陶文宪　侯小明　李公科　郭继孚

　　　　　乔晓军　康云霞　仝　进

编辑工作人员

总   编   辑：孙中阁
编辑部主任：冯　杰
编辑部副主任：许国华
主编人员：万　颖　徐婧芸　宫秀青　徐瑞光　赵倩阳
编辑人员（按姓氏笔画排序）：

王　哲	王　薇	王晓磊	王望雄	王靖静	王澜润
石建南	白秀龙	成　浩	乔学礼	刘　宇	刘　远
刘　睿	刘宇环	刘明霞	刘　晨	刘滢锴	孙志国
曲孝利	纪　红	李　康	李　静	李　帅	李　扬
李　芳	李艳霞	李　颖	杨　雪	杨子帆	杨林立
吴志才	吴　颖	佟　乐	沈兴华	张　寅	张　旸
武锦坤	林　青	周华铮	周瑜芳	郑晓彬	郑爱清
单　颖	缐云飞	赵永振	赵　峰	郝庆玲	侯晓鹏
姜绍武	耿文康	高宏宇	高　蕾	黄　晨	黄　蓉
曹树辉	隋丽娜	董升伟	蔡苗青	樊会晓	隰文博

编 者 说 明

一、为全面反映北京市交通行业发展状况，方便社会各界了解北京市交通建设与发展现状，北京市交通委员会组织编辑了本资料，供广大读者作为资料性书籍使用。

二、本资料收录了 2018 年北京市交通运输主要统计指标数据，正文内容具体包括交通运输主要指标、公路、城市道路、旅客运输、货物运输、路网运行、附录共七篇。每篇由简要说明、统计表和主要指标解释组成。简要说明在每章节首页，简要概述本部分的主要内容、资料来源、统计范围等。统计表是各章节的核心内容。主要指标解释在每篇页尾，主要对本篇涉及的主要指标及其计算方法做出简要解释和说明。

三、本资料的统计数据主要由北京市交通委员会统计汇编形成。

四、本资料中，部分数据的合计数和相对数由于小数位取舍不同而产生的计算误差未做调整。

五、本资料的符号使用说明：

"-" 表示该项数据为零，或没有该项数据，或该项数据不详。

北京市交通委员会

2019 年 6 月

NOTES FROM EDITORS

Ⅰ. In order to fully reflect the development of Beijing transportation industry, and to facilitate all circles to understand the current situation of transportation construction and development of Beijing, the Beijing Municipal Commission of Transport organized and edited this Yearbook as a reference book for readers.

Ⅱ. This Yearbook contains the main statistical indicator data of Beijing transportation in 2016. The main contents include seven chapters, i.e. Main Transportation Indicators, Highway, Urban Road, Passenger Transportation, Freight Transportation, Road Network and Appendix. Each chapter is composed of the Brief Introduction, Statistical Tables and Explanatory Notes to Main Indicators. The first page of each chapter is Brief Introduction, an overview of the main content, source of data, statistical scope of each chapter. Statistical Tables are the core content of each chapter. The last page of each chapter is Explanatory Notes to Main Indicators, mainly giving a brief explanation and introduction to the main indicators and calculation methods involved in this chapter.

Ⅲ. The statistical data in this Yearbook is mainly collected and compiled by the Beijing Municipal Commission of Transport.

Ⅳ. In this Yearbook, calculation error of the total and relative numbers of some data due to different decimal choice has not undergone adjustment.

Ⅴ. Symbol instructions of this Yearbook :

"-" means that the figure is zero, unavailable, or unkown.

Beijing Municipal Committee of Transport

2019.6

目　录 CONTENTS

一、交通运输主要指标 MAIN TRANSPORTATION INDICATORS

　　简要说明···（2）
　　　　Brief Introduction
　1-1　国民经济主要指标···（3）
　　　　Main National Economy Indicators
　1-2　交通运输主要指标···（4）
　　　　Main Transportation Indicators

二、公路 HIGHWAY

　　简要说明···（6）
　　　　Brief Introduction
　2-1　公路密度情况··（7）
　　　　Statistics on Highway Density
　2-2　公路里程（按行政区划分）··（8）
　　　　Length of Highway (By Administrative Divisions)
　2-3　公路里程（按技术等级分）··（10）
　　　　Length of Highway (By Technical Level)
　2-4　公路里程（按路面类型分）··（11）
　　　　Length of Highway (By Pavement Materials)
　2-5　公路桥梁（按行政区划分）··（12）
　　　　Statistics on Highway Bridge (By Administrative Divisions)
　2-6　公路桥梁（按跨径分）··（14）
　　　　Statistics on Highway Bridge (By Span)
　2-7　公路隧道···（14）
　　　　Highway Tunnel
　2-8　高速公路明细情况···（16）
　　　　Schedule of Expressway
　2-9　国道明细情况··（18）
　　　　Schedule of National Highway

2-10　省道明细情况 ·· (19)
　　　　　Schedule of Beijing Provincial Expressway
　　　　主要统计指标解释 ·· (23)
　　　　　Explanatory Notes on Main Statistical Indicators

三、城市道路 URBAN ROAD

　　　　简要说明 ·· (26)
　　　　　Brief Introduction
　　3-1　城区各环路内道路密度情况 ·· (27)
　　　　　Statistics on Road Density within Urban Ring Roads
　　3-2　城市道路（按行政区划分）·· (28)
　　　　　Urban Roads (By Administrative Divisions)
　　3-3　城市道路基本情况 ··· (28)
　　　　　Basic Statistics on Urban Roads
　　3-4　城市快速路明细情况 ·· (30)
　　　　　Schedule of Rapid Roads
　　3-5　城市主干路明细情况 ·· (31)
　　　　　Schedule of Urban Main Roads
　　　　主要统计指标解释 ·· (47)
　　　　　Explanatory Notes on Main Statistical Indicators

四、旅客运输 PASSENGER TRANSPORTATION

　　　　简要说明 ·· (50)
　　　　　Brief Introduction
　　4-1　轨道交通 ··· (51)
　　　　　Rail Transit
　　4-2　轨道交通分线路运营情况 ·· (52)
　　　　　Operation of Rail Transit by Line
　　4-3　前五位轨道交通站点及线路 ··· (53)
　　　　　Top 5 Rail Transit Stations and Lines
　　4-4　轨道交通运营线路换乘站 ·· (54)
　　　　　Transfer Station of Rail Transit Operating Lines
　　4-5　公共电汽车 ·· (56)
　　　　　Public Trolley Buses
　　4-6　出租汽车 ··· (58)
　　　　　Taxi
　　4-7　省际客运 ··· (59)
　　　　　Interprovincial Passenger Transportation
　　4-8　旅游客运 ··· (60)
　　　　　Tourist Passenger Transportation

4-9 郊区客运 ......（61）
　　Suburban Passenger Transportation
4-10 公路营运载客汽车拥有量 ......（62）
　　Possession of Commercial Highway Passenger Vehicles
4-11 汽车租赁 ......（64）
　　Vehicle Rental
4-12 机动车维修业及汽车综合性能检测站 ......（65）
　　Motor Vehicle Maintenance and Synthetic Vehicle Performance Test Station
　　主要统计指标解释 ......（66）
　　Explanatory Notes on Main Statistical Indicators

五、货物运输 FREIGHT TRANSPORTATION

　　简要说明 ......（76）
　　Brief Introduction
5-1 货物运输 ......（77）
　　Freight Transportation
5-2 公路货物营运车辆拥有量（按标记吨位分）......（78）
　　Possession of Commercial Highway Freight Vehicles (By Capacity Tonnage)
5-3 公路货物营运车辆拥有量（按总质量分）......（80）
　　Possession of Commercial Highway Freight Vehicles (By Total Mass)
　　主要统计指标解释 ......（82）
　　Explanatory Notes on Main Statistical Indicators

六、路网运行 ROAD NETWORK

　　简要说明 ......（84）
　　Brief Introduction
6-1 公路交通调查管理情况 ......（85）
　　Highway Traffic Survey Management
6-2 国家高速公路交通量 ......（86）
　　National Expressway Traffic
6-3 普通国道交通量 ......（88）
　　Ordinary National Highway Traffic
6-4 普通省道交通量 ......（90）
　　Ordinary Provincial Highway Traffic
　　主要统计指标解释 ......（94）
　　Explanatory Notes on Main Statistical Indicators

七、附录 APPENDIX

7-1 北京、天津、河北、上海公路基本情况 ......（99）
　　Highway of Beijing&Tianjin&Hebei&Shanghai

7-2　全国公路里程（按行政等级分）···（100）
　　　Length of Nationwide Highway (By Administrative Level)

7-3　全国公路里程（按技术等级分）···（101）
　　　Length of Nationwide Highway (By Technical Level)

7-4　全国高速公路里程···（102）
　　　Length of Nationwide Expressway

7-5　全国公路密度及通达率···（103）
　　　Density and Service Rate of Nationwide Highway

7-6　全国公路客、货运输量···（104）
　　　Passenger and Freight Traffic of Nationwide Highway

7-7　全国城市客运设施···（105）
　　　National Urban Passenger Transport Facilities

7-8　全国公共汽电车客运量···（106）
　　　National Public Trolley Buses Traffic Volume

7-9　全国轨道交通运量···（107）
　　　National Rail Transit Traffic Volume

7-10　全国出租汽车运量···（108）
　　　National Taxi Traffic Volume

一、交通运输主要指标
MAIN TRANSPORTATION INDICATORS

简 要 说 明
Brief Introduction

本篇资料反映北京市国民经济和交通运输的主要指标。

国民经济主要指标包括：人口、地区生产总值、财政收入支出、固定资产投资、能源消费等，来源于《北京市统计年鉴》

交通运输主要指标包括：交通基础设施投资、公路运输、城市客运、机动车保有量、路网运行等。

Statistics in this chapter include main indicators of national economy and transportation of Beijing.

National economic indicators include population, GDP, government finance, investment in fixed assets, energy consumption and so on, mainly from *Beijing Statistical Yearbook*.

Transport indicators include investment in transportation infrastructure, highway transport, urban passenger transport, road network and so on.

1-1　国民经济主要指标
Main National Economy Indicators

指标 Indicator		计量单位 Unit		数量 Number
人口	Population	-	-	-
年末常住人口	Permanent Population (year-end)	万人	10 000 persons	2 154.2
年末户籍人口	Registered Population (year-end)	万人	10 000 persons	1 375.8
国民经济核算	National Accounts	-	-	-
地区生产总值（GDP）	Gross Domestic Product	亿元	100 million yuan	30 320.0
第一产业	Primary Industry	亿元	100 million yuan	118.7
第二产业	Secondary Industry	亿元	100 million yuan	5 647.7
第三产业	Tertiary Industry	亿元	100 million yuan	24 553.6
财政	Government Finance	-	-	-
一般公共预算收入	Local Public Budgetary Revenue	亿元	100 million yuan	5 785.9
一般公共预算支出	Local Public Budgetary Expenditure	亿元	100 million yuan	6 406.8
固定资产投资	Investment in Fixed Assets	-	-	-
全社会固定资产投资增速	Total Investment in Fixed Assets Year-on-year Growth Rate	%	%	-9.9
其中：交通领域	of which: Transportation Investment	亿元	100 million yuan	752.9
价格指数（上年=100）	Price Index (Preceding Year = 100)	-	-	-
居民消费价格指数	Consumer Price Index	%	%	102.5
商品零售价格指数	Retail Price Index	%	%	101.1
能源消费总量增速	Total Energy Consumption Year-on-year Growth Rate	%	%	**2.6**

1-2 交通运输主要指标
Main Transportation Indicators

指标 Indicator		计量单位 Unit		数量 Number
综合指标	Comprehensive Indicator	—	—	—
中心城交通指数	Traffic Index of Inner City	—	—	5.5
中心城绿色出行比例	Green Travel Ratio of Inner City	%	%	73.0
机动车保有量	Number of Motor Vehicles	万辆	10 000 vehicles	608.4
交通基础设施	Transportation Infrastructure	—	—	—
境内道路总里程	Total Length of Highway and Roads	公里	km	29 429
公路里程	Total Length of Highway	公里	km	22 256
其中：高速公路	of which: Expressway	公里	km	1 115
公路桥梁	Highway Bridges	米/座	meter/bridge	673 475/6 677
公路隧道	Highway Tunnels	米/处	meter/tunnel	102 552/135
公路网密度	Highway Network Density	公里/百平方公里	km/100 square kms	135.62
城市道路里程	Length of Urban Roads	公里	km	6 203
其中：快速路	of which: Rapid Roads	公里	km	390
城市桥梁	Urban Bridges	座	unit	2 156
城市立交桥系	Urban Flyovers	个	unit	435
轨道交通运营线路长度	Rail Transit Operation Line Length	公里	km	636
轨道交通车站	Rail Transit Station	个	unit	391
其中：换乘站	of which: Transfer Station	个	unit	59
公共电汽车停车保养场	Buses and Trolley Buses Parking Lots	个	unit	677
公交专用道长度	Bus Lane Length	公里	km	952
客货运输	Passenger and Freight Transportation	—	—	—
公路载客汽车	Highway Passenger Vehicles	辆	vehicle	75 262
公路载货汽车	Highway Freight Vehicles	辆	vehicle	168 626
公路客运量	Highway Passenger Traffic	万人次	10 000 person-times	44 175
公路旅客周转量	Highway Passenger Turnover	万人公里	10 000 person-kms	993 699
公路货运量	Highway Freight Traffic	万吨	10 000 tons	20 278
公路货物周转量	Highway Freight Turnover	万吨公里	10 000 ton-kms	1 674 068
轨道交通客运量	Rail Transit Passenger Traffic	万人次	10 000 person-times	384 843
轨道交通最高日客运量	Maximum Daily Passenger Traffic of Rail Transit	万人次	10 000 person-times	1 349
公共电汽车客运量	Buses and Trolley Buses Passenger Traffic	万人次	10 000 person-times	318 975
公共电汽车最高日客运量	Maximum Daily Passenger Traffic of Buses and Trolley Buses	万人次	10 000 person-times	1 170
出租汽车客运量	Taxi Passenger Traffic	万人次	10 000 person-times	34 021

二、公　　路
HIGHWAY

简 要 说 明
Brief Introduction

一、本篇资料反映北京市公路基础设施发展的基本情况。主要包括：公路密度、公路里程、公路桥梁、公路隧道等统计数据。

Ⅰ. Statistics in this chapter reflect the basic situation of highway infrastructure in Beijing, mainly including statistical data of highway density, highway length, highway bridges, highway tunnels and so on.

二、公路里程为年末通车里程，不含在建和未正式投入使用的公路里程。

Ⅱ. The length of highway is the traffic mileage at the end of 2018, excluding the highway mileage under construction or not formally put into use.

2-1 公路密度情况
STATISTICS on Highway Density

行政区划 Administrative Division		公路密度 （公里/百平方公里） Highway Density （km/100 sq. kms）	公路里程 （公里） Highway Length （km）
门头沟区	Mentougou District	67.7	982
房山区	Fangshan District	158.0	3 144
通州区	Tongzhou District	281.8	2 554
顺义区	Shunyi District	289.1	2 949
昌平区	Changping District	143.5	1 928
大兴区	Daxing District	279.4	2 896
怀柔区	Huairou District	79.0	1 677
平谷区	Pinggu District	174.6	1 659
密云区	Miyun District	95.2	2 122
延庆区	Yanqing District	96.9	1 932

2-2 公路里程
Length of Highway

行政区划 Administrative Divisions		里程总计 Total Mileage	国道 National Highway	国高 National Expressway	省道 Provincial Highway	县道 County Highway
合计	Total	22 256	1 921	683	2 025	3 856
东城区	Dongcheng District	–	–	–	–	–
西城区	Xicheng District	10	10	–	–	–
朝阳区	Chaoyang District	170	65	15	105	–
丰台区	Fengtai District	102	47	29	55	–
石景山区	Shijingshan District	8	–	–	8	–
海淀区	Haidian District	122	71	38	51	–
门头沟区	Mentougou District	982	179	19	73	254
房山区	Fangshan District	3 144	300	90	129	603
通州区	Tongzhou District	2 554	203	120	169	304
顺义区	Shunyi District	2 949	68	43	327	504
昌平区	Changping District	1 928	112	94	281	328
大兴区	Daxing District	2 896	198	103	172	414
怀柔区	Huairou District	1 677	219	13	89	321
平谷区	Pinggu District	1 659	43	–	217	310
密云区	Miyun District	2 122	245	81	118	398
延庆区	Yanqing District	1 932	160	39	231	419

（按行政区划分）
(By Administrative Divisions)

单位：公里　Unit:km

乡道 Township Highway	专用公路 Special Highway	村道 Village Highway	按技术等级分 By Technical Level				
			高速公路 Expressway	一级公路 Class I	二级公路 Class II	三级公路 Class III	四级公路 Class IV
7 537	1 350	5 568	1 115	1 457	4 029	3 970	11 685
–	–	–	–	–	–	–	–
–	–	–	2	8	–	–	–
–	–	–	122	37	11	–	–
–	–	–	47	8	48	–	–
–	–	–	8	–	–	–	–
–	–	–	89	21	13	–	–
254	60	162	19	41	230	276	417
968	255	890	100	137	559	592	1 755
1 141	167	570	165	318	462	297	1 311
886	238	925	91	178	599	524	1 558
807	83	317	133	137	344	393	922
1 006	203	902	147	143	488	385	1 733
555	99	395	19	162	243	422	831
570	123	395	26	90	367	197	978
727	91	543	81	107	276	475	1 184
622	31	469	66	70	391	409	996

2-3 公路里程（按技术等级分）
Length of Highway (By Technical Level)

单位：公里　Unit:km

指标 Indicator	公路里程总计 Total	等级公路 Classified Highway								
		合计 Total	高速公路 Expressway			八车道及以上 Eight-Lane and above	一级 Class I	二级 Class II	三级 Class III	四级 Class IV
			小计 Subtotal	四车道 Four-Lane	六车道 Six-Lane					
合计 Total	22 256	22 256	1 115	507	539	68	1 457	4 029	3 970	11 685
国道 National Highway	1 921	1 921	768	393	340	34	437	545	171	—
其中：国家高速公路 of which: National Expressway	683	683	683	359	292	31	—	—	—	—
省道 Provincial Highway	2 025	2 025	347	114	199	34	498	1 029	150	—
县道 County Highway	3 856	3 856	—	—	—	—	356	1 223	2 150	126
乡道 Township Highway	7 537	7 537	—	—	—	—	129	486	987	5 934
专用公路 Special Highway	1 350	1 350	—	—	—	—	26	654	245	425
村道 Village Highway	5 568	5 568	—	—	—	—	11	92	266	5 199

2-4 公路里程（按路面类型分）
Length of Highway (By Pavement Materials)

单位：公里 Unit:km

指标 Indicator		公路里程总计 Total	有铺装路面（高级） Paved Road (High-Type)			简易铺装路面 （次高级） Simple Pavement (Sub-high Type)	未铺装路面 （中级、低级、无路面） Unpaved (Intermediate Type, Low Type, No Pavement)
			合计 Total	沥青混凝土 Asphalt Concrete Pavement	水泥混凝土 Cement Concrete Pavement		
合　计	Total	22 256	22 256	17 452	4 804	-	-
国道	National Highway	1 921	1 921	1 921	-	-	-
其中：国家高速公路	of which: National Expressway	683	683	683	-	-	-
省道	Provincial Highway	2 025	2 025	2 022	3	-	-
县道	County Highway	3 856	3 856	3 802	54	-	-
乡道	Township Highway	7 537	7 537	5 542	1 995	-	-
村道	Village Highway	5 568	5 568	2 947	2 622	-	-
专用公路	Special Highway	1 350	1 350	1 219	131	-	-

2-5 公路桥梁
STATISTICS on Highway Bridge

行政区划 Administrative Divisions		总计 Total		其中：互通式立交 of which: Multi-passing Grade Separation	
		座 Number	延米 Meter	座 Number	延米 Meter
合 计	Total	**6 677**	**673 475**	**158**	**61 093**
朝阳区	Chaoyang District	216	49 133	18	11 921
丰台区	Fengtai District	127	12 225	4	611
石景山区	Shijingshan District	20	5 404	2	1 089
海淀区	Haidian District	125	30 941	6	1 315
门头沟区	Mentougou District	235	25 185	7	1 023
房山区	Fangshan District	846	80 573	9	1 756
通州区	Tongzhou District	918	90 168	14	5 932
顺义区	Shunyi District	658	49 706	18	6 696
昌平区	Changping District	618	61 135	11	4 366
大兴区	Daxing District	679	79 489	35	20 715
怀柔区	Huairou District	634	59 768	4	708
平谷区	Pinggu District	363	22 150	3	598
密云区	Miyun District	763	60 385	17	2 541
延庆区	Yanqing District	475	47 214	10	1 823

二、公 路

（按行政区划分）
(By Administrative Divisions)

按桥梁长度分类 By Length of Bridge							
特大桥 Special Large-size Bridge		大桥 Large-size Bridge		中桥 Medium-size Bridge		小桥 Small-size Bridge	
座 Number	延米 Meter	座 Number	延米 Meter	座 Number	延米 Meter	座 Number	延米 Meter
101	**204 562**	**1 051**	**288 023**	**1997**	**117 321**	**3 528**	**63 569**
9	23 409	58	19 597	80	4 936	69	1 191
–	–	28	8 461	40	2 629	59	1 135
2	2 371	6	2 610	6	298	6	126
10	15 488	44	12 073	47	2 956	24	424
4	12 218	31	6 274	78	4 651	122	2 043
5	6 591	155	52 296	243	13 617	443	8 069
16	32 433	129	33 691	213	13 402	560	10 642
6	12 468	73	18 335	225	12 002	354	6 900
12	16 677	97	24 405	249	15 594	260	4 458
16	43 807	69	15 730	223	12 825	371	7 128
6	15 232	111	30 029	163	8 773	354	5 734
2	2 165	51	10 110	110	6 313	200	3 562
1	1 485	139	38 632	189	12 578	434	7 690
12	20 219	60	15 780	131	6 748	272	4 468

2-6 公路桥梁
Statistics on Highway Bridge

指标 Indicator		桥梁总计 Total Bridgs			
		总计 Total		互通式 Multi-passing Grade Separation	
		座 Number	米 Meter	座 Number	米 Meter
合　计	Total	6 677	673 475	158	61 093
国道	National Highway	2 283	338 855	98	29 320
其中：国家高速公路	of which: National Expressway	1 651	269 966	82	26 668
省道	Provincial Highway	1 429	229 037	56	31 322
县道	County Highway	1 051	51 664	4	451
乡道	Township Highway	1 302	35 033	–	–
专用公路	Special Highway	92	6 262	–	–
村道	Village Highway	520	12 624	–	–

2-7 公　路
Highway

指标 Indicator		合计 Total		特长隧道 Extra-long Tunnel	
		米 Meter	处 Number	米 Meter	处 Number
合　计	Total	102 552	135	35 044	9
国道	National Highway	45 779	79	13 238	4
其中：国家高速公路	of which: National Expressway	22 176	33	6 448	2
省道	Provincial Highway	48 706	26	21 806	5
县道	County Highway	4 899	21	–	–
乡道	Township Highway	2 320	7	–	–
专用公路	Special Highway	848	2	–	–
村道	Village Highway	–	–	–	–

（按跨径分）
(By Span)

按跨径分 By Span							
特大桥 Special Large-size Bridge		大桥 Large-size Bridge		中桥 Medium-size Bridge		小桥 Small-size Bridge	
座 Number	米 Meter	座 Number	米 Meter	座 Number	米 Meter	座 Number	米 Meter
101	**204 562**	**1 051**	**288 023**	**1 997**	**117 321**	**3 528**	**63 569**
46	102 670	588	170 423	809	50 935	840	14 827
39	90 140	438	130 122	623	40 123	551	9 582
54	100 407	304	88 364	496	29 325	575	10 942
1	1 485	118	21 645	316	17 249	616	11 284
–	–	24	3 580	250	13 435	1 028	18 017
–	–	8	2 743	47	2 570	37	949
–	–	9	1 268	79	3 807	432	7 548

隧　道
Tunnel

长隧道 Long Tunnel		中隧道 Middle Tunnel		短隧道 Short Tunnel	
米 Meter	处 Number	米 Meter	处 Number	米 Meter	处 Number
37 841	**19**	**12 025**	**18**	**17 642**	**89**
14 314	8	6 204	9	12 023	58
8 806	5	600	1	6 322	25
22 447	10	3 304	5	1 149	6
–	–	1 897	3	3 002	18
1 080	1	–	–	1 240	6
–	–	620	1	228	1
–	–	–	–	–	–

2-8 高速公路明细情况
Schedule of Expressway

单位：公里　Unit:km

路线名称 Route Name	路线编号 Route Number	起讫地点 From /To	里程 Mileage
合计 total	—	—	1 114.6
京哈高速 Jingha Expressway	G1	四方桥西（四环）－大沙务（市界） Sifangqiao West (4th Ring Road) – Dashawu (City Boundary)	39.9
京沪高速 Jinghu Expressway	G2	十八里店桥（四环）－柴厂屯 Shibalidianqiao (4th Ring Road) – Chaichangtun	35.0
京台高速 Jingtai Expressway	G3	德贤桥（五环）－礼贤（河北界） Dexianqiao (5th Ring Road) – Lixian (Hebei Boundary)	27.2
京港澳高速 Beijing–Hong Kong–Macau Expressway	G4	六里桥（三环）－琉璃河（京冀界） Liuliqiao (3rd Ring Road) – Liuli River (Beijing–Hebei Boundary)	45.6
京昆高速 Jingkun Expressway	G5	京昆联络线－镇江营（京冀界） Jingkun Contact Line – Zhenjiangying (Beijing–Hebei Boundary)	40.4
京藏高速 Jingzang Expressway	G6	马甸桥（三环）－康庄（京冀界） Madianqiao (3rd Ring Road) – Kangzhuang (Beijing–Hebei boundary)	68.4
京新高速 Jingxin Expressway	G7	（五环）－德胜口隧道北口 (5th Ring Road) – Deshengkou Tunnel North	37.7
京新高速 Jingxin Expressway	G7	米家堡－（京冀界） Mijiapu – (Beijing–Hebei Boundary)	21.9
大广高速 Daguang Expressway	G45	司马台（京冀界）－新农村 Simatai (Beijing–Hebei Boundary) – Xinnongcun	62.7
		新农村－酸枣岭桥东 Xinnongcun – Suanzaolingqiao East	46.7
		酸枣岭桥东－酸枣岭桥（六环） Suanzaolingqiao East – Suanzaolingqiao (6th Ring Road)	0.7
		酸枣岭桥（六环）－双源桥（六环） Suanzaolingqiao (6th Ring Road) – Shuangyuanqiao (6th Ring Road)	—
		双源桥（六环）－辛立村立交 Shuangyuanqiao (6th Ring Road)–Xinlicun Flyover	15.3
		辛立村立交－固安大桥（京冀界） Xinlicun Flyover – Gu'an Bridge (Beijing–Hebei Boundary)	9.0
北京绕城高速 Beijing Ring Expressway	G4501	酸枣岭桥－酸枣岭桥 Suanzaolingqiao – Suanzaolingqiao	187.6
京秦高速 Jingqin Expressway	G0121	五环路－潮白河大桥 5th Ring Road – Chaobaihe Bridge	6.7
首都环线高速 Ring Road of Capital Area	G95	镇罗营－采育（市界） Zhenluoying – Yucai (Municipal Boundary)	38.2

2-8（续表一）

路线名称 Route Name	路线编号 Route Number	起讫地点 From /To	里程 Mileage
京抚线 Jingfu Line	G102	西马庄收费站－白庙（京冀界） Ximazhuang Toll Gate – Baimiao (Beijing–Hebei Boundary)	13.8
京滨线 Jingbin Line	G103	大望桥西－八里桥 Dawangqiao West–Baliqiao	12.9
京广线 Jingguang line	G106	菜户营（二环）－榆垡收费站 Caihuying (2nd Ring Road)–Yufa Toll Gate	22.7
京昆线 Jingkun Line	G108	复兴门（二环）－卧龙岗（六环） Fuxingmen (2nd Ring Road)–Wolonggang (6th Ring Road)	18.6
京拉线 Jingla line	G109	定慧桥（四环）－苹果园立交 Dinghuiqiao (4th Ring Road) – Pingguoyuan Flyover	14.6
京青线 Jingqing Line	G110	德胜门（二环）－马甸桥（三环） Deshengmen (2nd Ring Road) – Madianqiao (3rd Ring Road)	2.3
京承高速 Jingcheng Expressway	S11	望和桥（四环）－酸枣岭（六环） Wangheqiao (4th Ring Road) – Suanzaoling(6th Ring Road)	21.0
机场高速 Airport Express	S12	三元桥（三环）－首都机场（T2） Sanyuanqiao (3rd Ring Road) – Capital Airport (T2)	18.7
京津高速 Jingjin Expressway	S15	化工桥（五环）－永乐店（京冀界） Huagongqiao (5th Ring Road)–Yongledian (Beijing–Hebei Boundary)	34.1
机场北线 Airport North Line	S28	定泗路－机场 Dingsi Road–Airport	11.4
京平高速 Jingping Expressway	S32	京承高速－李天桥（六环） Jingcheng Expressway – Litianqiao (6th Ring Road)	17.5
京平高速 Jingping Expressway	S32	李天桥（六环）－大岭后隧道（京冀界） Litianqiao (6th Ring Road)–Dalinghou Tunnel (Beijing–Hebei Boundary)	52.8
京密高速 Jingmi Expressway	S35	京承高速－怀柔开放环岛 Jingcheng Expressway – Huairou Open Roundabout	6.1
京通京哈联络线 Jingtong Jingha Contact Line	S46	会村－西马庄 Huicun – Ximazhuang	3.2
五环路 5th Ring Road	S50	来广营立交－来广营立交 Laiguangying Flyover – Laiguangying Flyover	98.6
机场第二高速 Airport Second Expressway	S51	平房桥（五环）－岗山收费站（T3） Pingfangqiao (5th Ring Road) – Gangshan Toll Gate (T3)	15.8
京昆联络线 Jingkun Contact Line	S66	青龙湖收费站－京昆高速 Qinglonghu Toll Gate – Jingkun Expressway	10.8
京礼高速 Jingli Expressway	S3801	六环路－兴延崇分界点 6th Ring Road – Demarcation Point of Xingyan Expressway and Yanchong Expressway	41.8
京礼高速 Jingli Expressway	S3801	兴延崇分界点－G110国道 Demarcation Point of Xingyan Expressway and Yanchong Expressway – G110	15.1

注：1. 大广高速与六环路重合路段为六环路（酸枣岭—双源桥），里程为84.3公里。
2. 原京秦高速G1N根据国高编码改成G0121，且由干线改为联络线。平房桥（五环）－机场二高速段调整为机场第二高速。

Note: I. The length of 6th Ring Road (Suanzaolingqiao – Shuangyuanqiao) where Daguang Expressway and the 6th Ring Road coincide is 84.3 kilometers.
II. The original Jingqin Expressway G1N was changed to G0121 according to the national expressway code, and adjust to Airport Second Expressway because of the re-route of Pingfangqiao (5th Ring Road) – Airport Second Expressway section.

2-9 国道明细情况
Schedule of National Highway

路线名称 Route Name	路线编号 Route Number	起讫地点 From/To		里程（公里） Length (km)
合计 Total	—	—	—	1 920.7
国家高速 National Expressway				682.7
京哈高速 Jingha Expressway	G1	四方桥－香河	Sifangqiao－Xianghe	39.9
京秦高速 Jingqin Expressway	G0121	五环路－潮白河大桥	5th Ring Road－Chaobaihe Bridge	6.7
京沪高速 Jinghu Expressway	G2	十八里店桥（四环）－柴厂屯（京冀界）	Shibalidianqiao (4th Ring Road)－Chaichangtun (Beijing–Hebei boundary)	35.0
京台高速 Jingtai Expressway	G3	五环路－河北界	5th Ring Road－Hebei Boundary	27.2
京港澳高速 Jinggang'ao Expressway	G4	六里桥（三环）－琉璃河（京冀界）	Liuliqiao (3rd Ring Road)－Liulihe (Beijing–Hebei Boundary)	45.6
京昆高速 Jingkun Expressway	G5	G108－市界	G108–Municipal Boundary	40.4
京藏高速 Jingzang Expressway	G6	马甸桥（三环）－康庄（京冀界）	Madianqiao (3rd Ring Road)－Kangzhuang (Beijing–Hebei Boundary)	68.4
京新高速 Jingxin Expressway	G7	五环－京冀界	5th Ring Road－Beijing–Hebei Boundary	59.6
大广高速 Daguang Expressway	G45	京冀界－市界	Beijing–Hebei Boundary－Municipal Boundary	134.3
北京绕城高速 Beijing Ring Expressway	G4501	酸枣岭－酸枣岭	Suanzaoling－Suanzaoling	187.6
首都环线高速 Ring Expressway of Capital City	G95	镇罗营－采育（市界）	Zhenluoying－Caiyu (Municipal Boundary)	38.2
普通国道 Ordinary National Highway	—	—	—	1 237.9
京沈线 Jingshen Line	G101	东直门－市界	Dongzhimen－Municipal Boundary	124.0
京抚线 Jingfu Line	G102	朝阳门－市界燕郊	Chaoyangmen–Municipal Boundary Yanjiao	31.3
京滨线 Jingbin Line	G103	建国门－觅子店	Jianguomen－Mizidian	50.1
京岚线 Jinglan Line	G104	永定门－市界	Yongdingmen－Municipal Boundary	46.8
京澳线 Jing'ao Line	G105	永定门－市界	Yongdingmen－Municipal Boundary	0.0
京广线 Jingguang Line	G106	菜户营桥－市界	Caihuyingqiao－Municipal Boundary	44.3
京港线 Jinggang Line	G107	广安门－北京界（挟河桥）	Guang'anmen–Beijing Boundary (Xieheqiao)	39.2
京昆线 Jingkun Line	G108	复兴门－北京界	Fuxingmen–Beijing Boundary	133.5
京拉线 Jingla Line	G109	阜成门－大垭口（市界）	Fuchengmen－Dayakou (Municipal Boundary)	119.0
京青线 Jingqing Line	G110	德胜门－市界（下营）	Deshengmen－Municipal Boundary (Xiaying)	66.9
京漠线 Jingmo Line	G111	开放路环岛－市界	Kaifang Road Roundabout－Municipal Boundary	106.1
通武线 Tongwu Line	G230	市界－市界	Municipal Boundary－Municipal Boundary	91.4
兴阳线 Xingyang Line	G234	市界－易县（龙安大桥）	Municipal Boundary－Yi County (Long'an Bridge)	325.2
承塔线 Chengta Line	G335	二道梁－市界	Erdaoliang－Municipal Boundary	45.5
唐通线 Tingtong Line	G509	河北界－京塘线	Hebei Boundary–Jingtang Line	14.6

2-10 省道明细情况
Schedule of Beijing Provincial Expressway

路线名称 Route Name	路线编号 Route Number	起讫地点	起讫地点 From/To	里程（公里） Mileage (km)
合 计 Total	—	—	—	2 024.8
京承高速 Jingcheng Expressway	S11	土坡桥－酸枣岭（六环）	Tuchengqiao – Suanzaoling(6th Ring Road)	21.0
机场高速 Airport Expressway	S12	三元桥（三环）－首都机场	Sanyuanqiao (3rd Ring Road) – Capital Airport	18.7
京津高速 Jingjin Expressway	S15	化工路立交（五环）－京冀界	Huagong Road Flyover (5th Ring Road) – Beijing–Hebei boundary	34.1
机场北线 Airport North Line	S28	定润路－机场	Dingsi Road – Airport	11.4
京平高速 Jingping Expressway	S32	京承高速－大岭后隧道	Jingcheng Expressway – Dalinghou Tunnel	70.3
京密高速 Jingmi Expressway	S35	庙城－京沈线出口	Miaocheng – Jingshen Line Exit	6.1
京礼高速 Jingli Expressway	S3801	六环路－G110国道	6th Ring Road – G110	56.9
京通京哈联络线 Jingtong Jingha Contact Line	S46	会村－西马庄	Huicun – West Mazhuang	3.2
五环路 5th Ring Road	S50	来广营立交－来广营立交	Laiguangying Flyover – Laiguangying Flyover	98.6
机场第二高速 Airport Second Expressway	S51	五环－T3航站楼	5th Ring Road – T3 Terminal	15.8
京昆联络线 Jingkun Contact Line	S66	房山区界－京昆高速	Fangshan District Boundary – Jingkun Expressway	10.8
通顺路 Tongshun Road	S201	京哈线－昌金路	Jingha Line – Changjin Road	33.3
张采路 Zhangcai Road	S202	土桥－南刘庄	Tuqiao – South Liuzhuang	23.8
顺密路 Shunmi Road	S203	顺平路－新南路	Shunping Road – Xinnan Road	32.8
密三路 Misan Road	S204	新农村－三河界	Xinnongcun – Sanhe Boundary	49.4
密关路 Miguan Road	S205	新南路－G234	Xinnan Road – G234	24.7
平三路 Pingsan Road	S206	平谷－赵家务	Pinggu – Zhaojiawu	4.6
通清路 Tongqing Road	S207	G509－G103	G509 – G103	10.5

2-10（续表一）

路线名称 Route Name	路线编号 Route Number	起讫地点 From/To	里程（公里） Mileage (km)
石担路 Shidan Road	S209	石门营环岛－担礼 Shimenying Roundabout – Danli	17.1
三温路 Sanwen Road	S210	煤矿学校－灰口 Meikuang School – Huikou	11.2
斋幽路 Zhaiyou Road	S211	斋堂－河北界（幽州）Zhaitang – Hebei Boundary (Youzhou)	25.0
昌赤路 Changchi Road	S212	涧头－水库大坝 Jiantou – Reservoir Dam	78.7
安四路 Ansi Road	S213	安定门－四海 Andingmen – Sihai	84.5
壁富路 Bifu road	S214	富豪－李天路 Fuhao – Litian Road	9.0
京开辅路 Jingkai Side Road	S215	玉泉营－六环路 Yuquanying – 6th Ring Road	17.1
G6辅路 G6 Side Road	S216	马甸－人文大学 Madian – Renwen University	73.1
康张路 Kangzhang Road	S217	G234－古龙路 G234 – Gulong Road	13.0
温南路 Wennan Road	S218	海淀区界－南口环岛 Haidian District Boundary – Nankou Roundabout	16.1
南雁路 Nanyan Road	S219	南口－京拉线 Nankou – Jingla Line	41.1
延康路 Yankang Road	S220	延庆－铁路桥 Yanqing – Tieluqiao	6.8
孔兴路 Kongxing Road	S221	涧兴路－天津界 Huoxing Road – Tianjin Boundary	11.3
崔杏路 Cuixing Road	S222	崔家庄－杏园 Cuijiazhuang – Xingyuan	14.8
潭永路 Huoyong Road	S223	京塘线－河北界 Jingtang Line – Hebei Boundary	21.7
木燕路 Muyan Road	S224	木林－燕郊 Mulin – Yanjiao	25.6
机场东路 Airport East Road	S225	顺平路－李天路 Shunping Road – Litian Road	9.3
马朱路 Mazhu Road	S226	潭马路口－朱庄 Huoma Junction – Zhuzhuang	13.5
杨雁路 Yangyan Road	S227	京承高速收费口－国道111 Jingcheng Expressway Toll Gate – National Highway 111	11.6

2-10（续表二）

路线名称	Route Name	路线编号 Route Number	起迄地点	From/To	里程（公里） Mileage (km)
南中轴路	South Zhongzhou Road	S228	黄亦路－市界	Huangyi Road – Municipal Boundary	29.2
通怀路	Tonghuai Road	S229	G103－潞苑北大街	G103 – Luyuan North Street	11.4
平程路	Pingcheng Road	S230	平谷－程各庄	Pinggu – Chenggezhuang	33.6
平兴路	Pingxing Road	S231	平谷靠山集－兴隆界将军关	Pinggu Kaoshanji – Xinglongjie Jiangjun Gate	8.6
茹川路	Guichuan Road	S232	西拨子二号桥－米家堡桥	Xibozi No. 2 Bridge – Mijiapu Bridge	15.8
怀雁路	Huaiyan Road	S233	京密高速－范崎路	Jingmi Expressway – Fanqi Road	5.7
德贤路	Dexian Road	S234	四环－五环路	4th Ring Road – 5th Ring Road	5.3
八岭路	Bayu Road	S235	八里店－黑岭口	Balidian – Heiyukou	14.3
鲁坨路	Lutuo Road	S236	鲁坨路联接线－羊圈头村	Lutuo Road Contact Line – Yangquantou Village	7.1
徐尹路	Xuyin Road	S301	朝阳界－市界	Chaoyang Boundary – Municipal Boundary	10.9
通马路	Tongma Road	S302	果园环岛－光机电路口	Guoyuan Roundabout – Guangjidian Junction	12.2
早鲍路	Zaobao Road	S304	早立庄（区界）－G230	Zaolizhuang(District Boundary) – G230	12.7
顺平路	Shunping Road	S305	天北路－韩庄	Tianbei Road – Hanzhuang	64.0
武兴路	Wuxing Road	S306	京塘线－河北界	Jingtang Line – Hebei Boundary	8.4
刘田路	Liutian Road	S307	刘家铺－礼贤西口桥西	Liujiapu – Lixianxikouqiao West	16.9
怀长路	Huaichang Road	S308	庙城立交桥－昌赤路	Miaocheng Flyover – Changchi Road	45.9
滦赤路	Luanchi Road	S309	二道梁－市界	Erdaoliang – Municipal Boundary	63.1
密兴路	Mixing Road	S311	金山子路口－北沟	Jinshanzi Junction – Beigou	21.2
松曹路	Songcao Road	S312	松树峪－市界	Songshuyu – Municipal Boundary	38.7

2-10（续表三）

路线名称 Route Name	路线编号 Route Number	起迄地点 From/To		里程（公里） Mileage (km)
岳琉路	Yueliu Road	S313	岳各庄－琉璃河（环岛）	Yuegezhuang– Liuli River (Roundabout)	13.5
平蓟路	Pingji Road	S314	平谷－蓟州区界	Pinggu–Jizhou Boundary	23.6
京良路	Jingliang Road	S315	G106新发地－京港澳高速	G106 Xinfadi – Beijing–Hong Kong–Macau Expressway	18.0
兴良路	Xingliang Road	S316	黄村（京开西辅路）－京周路	Huangcun (Jingkai West Side Road)–Jingzhou Road	20.0
京周路	Jingzhou Road	S317	广安门－周口店	Guang'anmen – Zhoukoudian	48.2
良陀路	Liangtuo Road	S319	京周路（良乡）－坨里	Jingzhou Road – Tuoli	10.9
G108复线	G108 Double Line	S320	京昆线－贾峪口	Jingkun Line – Jiayukou	23.9
顺沙路	Shunsha Road	S321	右堤路－葛村	Youdi Road – Gecun	47.8
黄马路	Huangma Road	S322	黄村－马驹桥	Huangcun – Majuqiao	19.5
旧小路	Jiuxiao Road	S323	旧县－小鲁庄	Jiuxian County – Xiaolunzhuang	11.6
沙阳路	Shayang Road	S324	沙河－京密引水渠	Shahe – Jingmi Channel	10.5
八达岭路	Badaling Road	S325	林场－西拨子桥	Linchang – Xibozipao	7.5
大件路	Dajian Road	S326	京周路－房东路路口	Jingzhou Road – Fangdong Road Junction	10.8
定泗路	Dingsi Road	S327	定福皇庄－火沙路	Dingfuhuangzhuang – Huosha Road	20.1
良三路	Liangsan Road	S328	良乡（高速出口）－三福村	Liangxiang (Expressway Exit)–Sanfucun	21.8
黄亦路	Huangyi Road	S329	芦求路－西周路	Luqiu Road – Xizhou Road	24.4
昌金路	Changjin Road	S330	崔阿路－K79+481	Cui'a Road – K79+481	79.5
顺平南线	Shunping South Line	S331	机场东路－平三路	Airport East Road – Pingsan Road	42.8
龙塘路	Longtang Road	S332	机场东路－顺平南线	Airport East Road – Shunping South Line	27.5
白马路	Baima Road	S335	秦北路－杨杏路	Qinbei Road – Yangxing Road	45.5
兴亦路	Xingyi Road	S336	芦求路－四海庄	Luqiu Road – Sihaizhuang	17.7
北清路	Beiqing Road	S337	北安河路－七星路	Beianhe Road – Qixing Road	27.7

主要统计指标解释

公路里程：指报告期末，公路的实际长度。计量单位：公里。

统计范围：凡达到交通运输部《公路工程技术标准》(JTG B01—2003)规定的技术等级的公路（县、乡道中，含路基宽度≥4.5米或路面宽度≥3.5米路段的等外路线的里程；村道中，含路基宽度≥4.5米或路面宽度≥3.0米路段的等外路线的里程），均统计为公路里程。包括大、中城市的郊区公路，以及公路通过城镇（指县城、集镇）街道的里程数和公路桥梁长度、隧道长度、渡口的宽度以及分期修建的公路已验收交付使用的里程。

统计分组：

按公路行政等级分为国道、省道、县道、乡道、专用公路和村道里程。

按是否达到公路工程技术标准分为等级公路里程和等外公路里程。等级公路里程按技术等级分为高速公路、一级公路、二级公路、三级公路、四级公路里程。

按公路路面类型分为有铺装路面、简易铺装路面和未铺装路面公路里程。有铺装路面里程含沥青混凝土、水泥混凝土路面公路里程。

公路密度：指报告期末，一定区域内单位国土面积所拥有的公路里程数，计量单位：公里/百平方公里。

公路桥梁数量：指报告期末，公路桥梁的实际数量。计量单位：座。

计算方法：

(1) 对于上下行路线及带有辅道的路线，两幅路上同一断面的并行桥梁按两座桥计算。

(2) 由于路线的多次加宽，单幅路同一断面出现两座以上不同建设年代、不同结构形式、不同荷载等级的桥梁统计为一座桥梁。

(3) 互通式立交桥梁计为一座桥梁。

统计分组：（一般按以下方式分组）

(1) 按公路桥梁的建筑材料和使用年限分为：永久性桥梁、半永久性桥梁、临时性桥梁数量。

(2) 按桥梁的跨径分为：特大桥、大桥、中桥、小桥数量。

公路隧道数量：指报告期末，公路隧道的实际数量。计量单位：处。

统计分组：

按公路隧道长度分为特长隧道（长度>3 000米）、长隧道（3 000米≥长度>1 000米）、中隧道（1 000米≥长度>500米）、短隧道（长度≤500米）。

Explanatory Notes on Main Statistical Indicators

Highway length refers to the actual length of highway at the end of the report period. Unit: km.

Statistical scope: Such statistics apply for any highway (covering substandard highways with roadbed width of 4.5m and above or pavement width of 3.5m and above in county highway and township highway, substandard highways with roadbed width of 4.5m and above or pavement width of 3.0m and above in village highway) reaching the technical grade of ministry of Transport stated in *Highway Engineering Technical Standards (JTG B01—2003)*, including the mileage of highways in suburbs of middle and large cities, mileage of highways passing through streets in towns (counties and townships), length of highway bridges, length of tunnels, width of ferries, and mileage of highways constructed in several phases and put into use.

Generally grouped in the following ways:

Divided into length of national highway, provincial highway, county highway, township highway, special highway and village highway by administration level.

Divided into length of standard highway and substandard highway according to whether to achieve the highway engineering technical standards. Standard highway is divided into expressway, Class I highway, Class II highway, Class III highway and Class IV highway mileage by technical grade.

According to the types of road surface, there are paved road surface, simple paved road surface and unpaved road surface. Paved road surface includes asphalt concrete pavement and cement concrete pavement.

Highway density refers to the number of highway length owned by per unit area within a certain region at the end of the report period. Unit: km /100 sq. kms.

Number of highway bridges refers to the actual number of highway bridges at the end of the report period. Unit: bridge.

Calculating method:

(1) For the up and down routes and those with auxiliary roads, the parallel bridges with the same section of two roads are calculated as two bridges.

(2) Due to the multiple widening of routes, two or more bridges with different construction ages, different structural forms and different load levels in the same section of a single road are counted as one bridge.

(3) Interchange bridge is counted as one bridge.

Generally grouped in the following ways:

(1) Divided into permanent bridge, semi-permanent bridge and temporary bridge by building materials and service life.

(2) Divided into special large-size bridge, large-size bridge, medium-size bridge and small-size bridge by the bridge span.

Number of highway tunnels refers to the actual number of highway tunnels at the end of the report period. Unit: tunnel.

Generally grouped in the following ways:

Highway tunnels can be divided into extra-long tunnels (length > 3 000 m), long tunnels(3 000 m ≥ length > 1 000 m), medium tunnels (1 000 m ≥ length > 500 m)and short tunnels (length ≤ 500 m) by length.

三、城市道路
URBAN ROAD

简 要 说 明
Brief Introduction

一、本篇资料反映北京市城市道路基础设施的基本情况。主要包括：城市道路长度和面积、城市桥梁、立交桥、过街设施等统计数据。

二、北京市城市道路统计范围：东城区、西城区、朝阳区、海淀区、丰台区、石景山区行政区划范围内所有城市道路及其附属设施；超出城六区行政区划范围、纳入市交通委员会养护管理的部分城市道路及其附属设施；五环路和五环内高速公路及其附属设施（计入城市快速路）。

Ⅰ. Statistics in this chapter reflected the basic situation of urban road infrastructure of Beijing, including length and area of urban roads, urban bridges, flyovers, crossing facilities and so on.

Ⅱ.The statistical scope of urban roads in Beijing is: all urban roads and related ancillary facilities within the administrative divisions of Dongcheng District, Xicheng District, Chaoyang District, Haidian District, Fengtai District and Shijingshan District; urban roads and related ancillary facilities beyond the scope of these six districts but maintained by Beijing Municipal Commission of Transport; 5th Ring Road and Inner 5th Ring Highway and Its Affiliated Facilities (included in Urban Expressway).

3-1 城区各环路内道路密度情况
Statistics on Road Density within Urban Ring Roads

环路位置 Location	区域面积 （平方公里） Region Area (sq. km)	道路长度 （公里） Road length (km)	道路面积（万平方米） Road area (10 000 sq. m)	其中: 行车道面积 of which: Vehicle Lane	长度密度 （公里／平方公里） Length density (km/sq. km)	面积密度（万平方米／平方公里） Area density (10,000 sq. m/sq. km)	其中: 行车道面积密度 of which: Vehicle Lane
二环以内（含二环） Within 2nd Ring Road (including 2nd Ring Road)	63	741	1 150	863	11.8	18.3	13.8
三环以内（含三环） Within 3rd Ring Road (including 3rd Ring Road)	159	1 452	2 627	2 031	9.1	16.5	12.8
四环以内（含四环） Within 4th Ring Road (including 4th Ring Road)	302	2 305	4 589	3 655	7.6	15.2	12.1
五环以内（含五环） Within 5th Ring Road (including 5th Ring Road)	668	3 785	7 147	5 825	5.7	10.7	8.7

3-2 城市道路
Urban Roads

行政区划 Administrative Divisions		合计 Total		快速路 Rapid Road		
		长度（公里）Length (km)	面积（万平方米）Area (10 000 sq.m)	长度（公里）Length (km)	面积（万平方米）Area (10 000 sq.m)	其中：匝道面积 of which: Ramp
合 计	Total	6 139	10 130	347	1 180	202
东城区	Dongcheng District	408	691	18	58	9
西城区	Xicheng District	541	898	20	67	14
朝阳区	Chaoyang District	1 865	3 420	121	418	72
海淀区	Haidian District	1 609	2 562	87	278	37
丰台区	Fengtai District	1 464	2 114	79	286	53
石景山区	Shijingshan District	253	445	22	74	17

注：1. 城市道路面积包含路面面积、人行道面积、匝道面积。
　　2. 北京城市道路总里程 6203 公里，其中，城六区 6139 公里，另 64 公里为城六区快速路、主干路在郊区的延伸。

Notes: I. Urban road area includes area of road surface, sidewalks and ramp.
　　　II. The total length of urban roads is 6203 km, Among them, 6139 kilometers are located in the six districts of Beijing. The difference of 64 kilometers is

3-3 城市道路
Basic Statistics

指标 Indicator		道路 Road	
		长度（公里）Length (km)	面积（万平方米）Area (10 000 sq. ms)
合 计	Total	6 203	10 328
快速路	Rapid Road	390	1 336
主干路	Trunk Road	998	3 583
次干路	Secondary Trunk Road	632	1 500
支路及以下	Branch Road and below	4 183	3 909

（按行政区划分）
(By Administrative Divisions)

主干道 Trunk Road		次干道 Secondary Trunk Road		支路以下 Branch Road and below	
长度（公里）Length (km)	面积（万平米）Area (10 000 sq.m)	长度（公里）Length (km)	面积（万平米）Area (10 000 sq.m)	长度（公里）Length (km)	面积（万平米）Area (10 000 sq.m)
979	3 542	632	1 500	4 182	3 908
59	243	62	160	269	230
86	341	61	142	374	348
378	1 358	183	439	1 183	1 206
259	941	155	373	1 109	970
166	561	112	266	1 107	1 001
32	98	59	121	140	153

the extension of Beijing Sixth District Rapid Road and Trunk Road in the suburbs.

基本情况
on Urban Roads

步道 Sidewalk		桥梁数（座）Number of Bridges (bridge)	立交桥系（座）Flyover (bridge)	过街设施（座、处）Crossing Facilities (unit)	
长度（公里）Length (km)	面积（万平方米）Area (10 000 sq. ms)			天桥 Overpass	地道 Underpass
2 046	1 730	2156	435	545	214
–	–	–	–	–	–
590	624	–	–	–	–
411	374	–	–	–	–
1 045	732	–	–	–	–

3-4 城市快速路明细情况
Schedule of Rapid Roads

路线名称 Route Name		起讫地点 From/To		通车里程 （公里） Mileage (km)
合 计	Total	–	–	**390.3**
环 路	Ring Roads	–	–	**244.8**
二环路	2nd Ring Road	环路	Ring Road	32.7
三环路	3rd Ring Road	环路	Ring Road	48.3
四环路	4th Ring Road	环路	Ring Road	65.3
五环路	5th Ring Road	环路	Ring Road	98.6
放射线	Radial Roads	–	–	**145.5**
京承高速	Jingcheng Expressway	太阳宫桥（三环）－来广营桥（五环）	Taiyanggongqiao (3rd Ring Road) – Laiguangyingqiao (5th Ring Road)	5.4
机场高速	Airport Expressway	小街桥（二环）－五元桥（五环）	Xiaojieqiao (2nd Ring Road) – Wuyuanqiao (5th Ring Road)	8.4
通惠河北路	Tonghuihe North Road	东便门桥（二环）－远通桥（五环）	Dongbianmenqiao (2nd Ring Road) – Yuantongqiao (5th Ring Road)	9.3
京沈高速	Jingshen Expressway	四方桥（四环）－五方桥（五环）	Sifangqiao (4th Ring Road) – Wufangqiao (5th Ring Road)	5.1
京开高速	Jingkai Expressway	菜户营桥（二环）－西红门南桥（五环）	Caihuyingqiao (2nd Ring Road) – Xihongmenqiao (5th Ring Road)	10.1
莲花池东西路	East Lianhuachi West Road	天宁寺桥（二环）－漫水桥（永定河西）	Tianningsiqiao (2nd Ring Road) – Manshuiqiao (Yongdinghe West)	16.5
京藏高速	Jingzang Expressway	德胜门（二环）－上清桥（五环）	Deshengmen (2nd Ring Road) – Shangqingqiao (5th Ring Road)	8.9
京港澳高速	Jinggang'ao Expressway	六里桥（三环）－宛平桥（五环）	Liuliqiao (3rd Ring Road) – Wanpingqiao (5th Ring Road)	8.8
学院路	Xueyuan Road	西直门桥（二环）－学院桥（四环）	Xizhimenqiao (2nd Ring Road) – Xueyuanqiao (4th Ring Road)	4.6
京沪高速	Jinghu Expressway	分钟寺桥（三环）－大羊坊桥（五环）	Fenzhongsiqiao (3rd Ring Road) – Dayangfangqiao (5th Ring Road)	6.5
丰北路	Fengbei Road	丽泽桥（三环）－京港澳高速	Lizeqiao (3rd Ring Road) – Jinggang'ao Expressway	5.3
万泉河路	Wanquanhe Road	苏州桥（三环）－肖家河桥（五环）	Suzhouqiao (3rd Ring Road) – Xiaojiaheqiao (5th Ring Road)	5.3
紫竹路（西外大街）	Zizhu Road (Xiwai Street)	西直门桥（二环）－紫竹桥东天桥（三环）	Xizhimenqiao (2nd Ring Road) – Zizhuqiao East Flyover (3rd Ring Road)	4.0
阜石路	Fushi Road	定慧桥（四环）－双峪环岛	Dinghuiqiao (4th Ring Road) – Shuangyu Roundabout	15.1
蒲黄榆路	Puhuangyu Road	榴乡桥（四环）－旧宫新桥（五环）	Liuxiangqiao (4th Ring Road) – Jiugongxinwqiao (5th Ring Road)	5.5
姚家园路	Yaojiayuan Road	平房桥（五环）－机场二高速	Pingfang qiao (5th Ring Road) – Airport Second Expressway	3.9
广渠路	Guangqu Road	大郊亭桥（四环）－怡乐西路	Dajiaotingqiao (4th Ring Road) – Yile West Road	11.9
京昆联络线	Jingkun Rail Link	西五环－京港澳高速	West 5th Ring Road – Jinggang'ao Expressway	10.8

3-5 城市主干路明细情况
Schedule of Urban Main Roads

路线名称 Route Name		起点名称 From		终点名称 To		通车里程 （公里） Mileage (km)
合 计	Total	–	–	–	–	**997.9**
安定路	Anding Road	安慧桥立交	Anhuiqiao Flyover	安贞桥	Anzhenqiao	2.3
安定门外大街	Andingmen Outer Street	安贞桥	Anzhenqiao	安定门立交	Andingmen Flyover	2.2
安立路	Anli Road	区界	District Boundary	安慧桥	Anhuiqiao	7.1
安宁庄东路	Anningzhuang East Road	安宁庄路	Anningzhuang Road	小营西路	Xiaoying West Road	1.9
安宁庄东路新建段	New section of Anningzhuang East Road	东北旺北路	Dongbeiwang North Road	规划欧德宝南路	Oudebao South Road(Planning)	1.4
安翔北路	Anxiang North Road	北辰西路	Beichen West Road	八达岭高速	Badaling Expressway	1.0
奥林东路	Aolin East Road	奥林东桥	Aolin East Bridge	科荟路	Kehui Road	1.5
奥林西路	Aolin West Road	奥林西桥（五环）	Aolin West Bridge (5th Ring Road)	科荟路口北侧人行道处	Sidewalk of Kehui Road Crossing North	2.3
八家南北线	Bajia North-South Line	毛纺路	Maofang Road	月泉路	Yuequan Road	1.4
白云路	Baiyun Road	复兴门外大街	Fuxingmen Outer Street	莲花池东路	Lianhuachi East Road	1.1
白纸坊东街	Baizhifang East Street	菜市口大街	Caishikou Street	右安门内大街	You'anmen Inner Street	0.9
白纸坊西街	Baizhifang Wast Street	右安门内大街	You'anmen Street	广安门南街	Guang'anmen South Street	1.2
北辰东路	Beichen East Road	科荟路	Kehui Road	北四环辅路（外环）	Side Road of North 4th Ring Road (outer ring)	2.3
北辰东路西辅路	West Side Road of Beichen East Road	大屯北路	Datun North Road	慧忠路	Huizhong Road	1.1
北辰路	Beichen Road	北辰桥立交	Beichenqiao Flyover	安华桥立交	Anhuaqiao Flyover	2.4
北辰桥改造道路	Reconstruction Road of Beichenqiao	鸟巢	Bird's Nest	北土城东路	Beitucheng Road East	1.7
北辰西路	Beichen West Road	科荟路	Kehui Road	北土城西路	Beitucheng Road West	4.0
北蜂窝北路	Beifengwo North Road	玉渊潭南路	Yuyuantan South Road	复兴路	Fuxing Road	0.4
北蜂窝路	Beifengwo Road	复兴路	Fuxing Road	莲花池东路	Lianhuachi East Road	1.1
北宫路	Beigong Road	莲石路	Lianshi Road	射击场路（长辛店北一街）	Shejichang Road (Changxindian North First Street)	2.0
北湖渠路	Beihuqu Road	五环路	5th Ring Road	小营北路	Xiaoying North Road	2.5

3-5 （续表一）

路线名称 Route Name		起点名称 From		终点名称 To		通车里程 （公里） Mileage (km)
北京西站南路 （西客站南路）	Beijing West Railway Station South Road (West Passenger Station South Road)	广安路	Guang'an Road	丽泽路	Lize Road	2.4
北京站前街	Beijing Railway Station Front Street	建国门内大街	Jianguomen Inner Street	北京站前	Beijing Railway Station Front	0.4
北清路	Beiqing Road	京包路	Jingbao Road	北安河路	Bei'anhe Road	14.4
北太平庄道路	Beitaipingzhuang Road	北土城西路	Beitucheng West Road	北三环中路	North 3rd Ring Middle Road	1.1
北土城东路	Beitucheng East Road	京承高速	Jingcheng Expressway	北辰路	Beichen Road	3.7
北土城西路	Beitucheng West Road	北辰路	Beichen Road	学院路	Xueyuan Road	3.4
北辛安路	Beixin'an Road	金安桥（阜石路）	Jin'anqiao (Fushi Road)	石景山路	Shijingshan Road	2.1
北苑路	Beiyuan Road	安立路	Anli Road	太阳宫路	Taiyanggong Road	7.8
菜市口大街	Caishikou Street	骡马市大街	Luomashi Street	右外东滨河路	Youwaidongbinhe Road	2.1
长春桥路	Changchunqiao Road	西三环	West 3rd Ring Road	长春桥	Changchunqiao	1.2
长椿街	Changchun Street	宣武门西大街	Xuanwumen West Street	广安门内大街	Guang'anmen Inner Street	1.1
朝阳北路	Chaoyang North Road	通州区界	Tongzhou District Boundary	东大桥	Dongdaqiao	15.3
朝阳公园南路	Chaoyang Park South Road	东四环路	East 4th Ring Road	朝阳公园西路	Chaoyang Park West Road	1.4
朝阳路	Chaoyang Road	京通快速路	Jingtong Rapid Road	京广桥	Jingguangqiao	14.5
朝阳门内大街	Chaoyangmen Inner Street	朝阳门立交	Chaoyangmen Flyover	东四路口	Dongsi Crossing	1.5
朝阳门外大街	Chaoyangmen Outer Street	京广桥	Jingguangqiao	朝阳门立交	Chaoyangmen Flyover	2.3
车公庄大街	Chegongzhuang Street	官园桥	Guanyuanqiao	三里河路	Sanlihe Road	1.9
车公庄西路	Chegongzhuang West Road	三里河路	Sanlihe Road	花园桥	Huayuanqiao	2.0
成寿寺路	Chengshousi Road	南三环东路	South 3rd Ring Road East	亦庄北环	Yizhuang North Ring	7.6
崇文门东大街	Chongwenmen East Street	东便门立交	Dongbianmen Flyover	崇文门路口	Chongwenmen Crossing	1.5

3-5 （续表二）

路线名称 Route Name		起点名称 From		终点名称 To		通车里程 （公里） Mileage (km)
崇文门内大街	Chongwenmen Inner Street	东长安街	East Chang'an Street	崇文门路口	Chongwenmen Crossing	0.8
崇文门外大街	Chongwenmen Outer Street	崇文门	Chongwenmen	天坛路	Tiantan Road	1.5
崇文门西大街	Chongwenmen West Street	崇内大街	Chongwenmen Inner Street	台基厂大街	Taijichang Street	0.6
大屯路	Datun Road	北苑路	Beiyuan Road	八达岭高速辅路	Side Road of Badaling Expressway	4.0
地安门东大街	Di'anmen East Street	美术馆后街	Meishuguan Back street	地外大街	Dianmen Outer Street	1.1
地安门西大街	Di'anmen West Street	地安门外大街	Di'anmen Outer Street	新街口南大街	Xinjiekou South Street	2.0
东长安街	East Chang'an Street	东单路口	Dongdan Crossing	广场西侧路	Guangchang West Side Road	1.9
东大桥路	Dongdaqiao Road	朝阳门外大街	Chaoyangmen Outer Street	建国门外大街	Jianguomen Outer Street	1.6
东单北大街	Dongdan North Street	金鱼胡同	Jinyu Hutong	东长安街	East Chang'an Street	0.8
东蒲立交北滨河路	Dongpu Flyover Beibinhe Road	游乐园南门	Youleyuan South Gate	天坛东路	Tiantan East Road	0.4
东四北大街	Dongsi North Street	北新桥路口	Beixinqiao Crossing	东四路口	Dongsi Crossing	1.8
东四南大街	Dongsi South Street	东四路口	Dongsi Crossing	金鱼胡同	Jinyu Hutong	1.0
东四十条	Dongsi shitiao	十条立交	Shitiao Flyover	东四北大街	Dongsi North Street	1.5
东苇路	Dongwei Road	机场辅路	Airport Side Road	朝阳路	Chaoyang Road	14.0
东直门内大街	Dongzhimen Inner Street	东直门立交	Dongzhimen Flyover	北新桥路口	Beixinqiao Crossing	1.5
东直门外大街	Dongzhimen Outer Street	东三环北路	East 3rd Ring Road North	东直门立交	Dongzhimen Flyover	2.4
东直门外斜街	Dongzhimen Outer Byway	新东路	Xindong Road	东直门外大街	Dongzhimen Outer Street	1.0
丰台东大街	Fengtai East Street	丰台北路	Fengtai North Road	七里庄路	Qilizhuang Road	0.8
丰葆路	Fengbao Road	丰草河	Fengcao River	樊羊路	Fanyang Road	2.3
复兴路	Fuxing Road	木樨地桥	Muxidiqiao	玉泉路	Yuquan Road	7.0
复兴门内大街	Fuxingmen Inner Street	西单	Xidan	复兴门桥	Fuxingmenqiao	1.5
复兴门外大街	Fuxingmen Outer Street	复兴门桥	Fuxingmenqiao	木樨地桥	Muxidiqiao	1.8

3-5 （续表三）

路线名称	Route Name	起点名称	From	终点名称	To	通车里程（公里）Mileage (km)
阜成路	FuCheng Road	三里河路	Sanlihe Road	定慧桥	Dinghuiqiao	5.1
阜成门内大街	Fuchengmen Inner Street	西四	Xisi	阜成门立交桥	Fuchengmen Flyover	1.5
阜成门外大街	Fuchengmen Outer Street	阜成门桥	Fuchengmenqiao	三里河路	Sanlihe Road	1.8
阜通东大街	Futong East Street	阜安路	Fu'an Road	北四环东路	North 4th Ring Road East	2.4
富丰路	Fufeng Road	科兴路	Kexing Road	外环西路	Outer Ring Road West	0.6
高梁桥路	Gaoliangqiao Road	学院南路	Xueyuan South Road	北展北街	Beizhan North Street	2.8
工人体育场北路	Workers Stadium North Road	长虹桥	Changhongqiao	十条立交	Shitiao Flyover	2.3
工人体育场东路	Workers Stadium East Road	工人体育场北路	Workers Stadium North Road	东大桥	Dongdaqiao	1.2
鼓楼外大街	Gulou Outer Street	安华桥立交	Anhuaqiao Flyover	鼓楼立交桥	Gulou Flyover	2.2
光明路	Guangming Road	光明桥	Guangming qiao	左安门内大街	Zuo'anmen Inner Street	1.0
广安路	Guang'an Road	湾子路口	Wanzi Crossing	西四环南路	West 4th Ring Road South	4.5
广安门内大街	Guang'anmen Inner Street	菜市口	Caishikou	广安门桥	Guang'anmen Bridge	2.2
广安门外大街	Guang'anmen Outer Street	广安门桥	Guang'anmen qiao	湾子路口	Wanzi Crossing	1.9
广莲路	Guanglian Road	南蜂窝路	Nanfengwo Road	西客站南广场	West Railway Station South Square	0.7
广渠路	Guangqu Road	高碑店路	Gaobeidian Road	三环路	3rd Ring Road	5.5
广渠路（快速路）	Guangqu Road (Rapid Road)	怡乐西路	Yile West Road	高碑店路	Gaobeidian Road	8.8
广渠门内大街	Guangqumen Inner Street	广渠门桥	Guangqumenqiao	崇文门外大街	Chongwenmen Outer Street	2.2
广渠门外大街	Guangqumen Outer Street	双井桥	Shuangjingqiao	广渠门桥	Guangqumenqiao	1.5
广顺北大街	Guangshun North Street	广顺桥	Guangshunqiao	阜通西大街	Futong West Street	2.6
广顺南大街	Guangshun South Street	阜通西大街	Futong West Street	京顺路	Jingshun Road	1.4
广泽路	Guangze Road	荣达路	Rongda Road	阜安西路	Fu'an West Road	1.3
和平里西街	Hepingli West Street	和平西桥	Hepingxiqiao	北二环	North 2nd Ring Road	2.4
红坊路	Hongfang Road	博大路	Boda Road	小红门路	Xiaohongmen Road	2.4

3-5 （续表四）

路线名称 Route Name		起点名称 From		终点名称 To		通车里程 （公里） Mileage (km)
湖光中街	Huguang Middle Street	广顺北大街	Guangshun North Street	南湖渠西路	Nanhuqu West Road	1.3
虎坊路	Hufang Road	骡马市大街	Luomashi Street	北纬路	Beiwei Road	0.7
花园东路	Huayuan East Road	北四环中路	North 4th Ring Middle Road	北土城西路	Beitucheng West Road	1.2
化工路北段	North section of Huagong Road	窑洼湖桥	Yaowahuqiao	京沈高速	Jingshen Expressway	2.5
化工路南段	South Section of Huagong Road	京沈高速	Jingshen Expressway	五环	5th Ring Road	4.1
槐房西路南延	South Extension of Huaifang West Road	西红门路	Xihongmen Road	春和路	Chunhe Road	2.5
黄楼路	Huanglou Road	康营东路	Kangying East Road	黄港桥	Huanggangqiao	6.6
慧忠路	Huizhong Road	北苑路	Beiyuan Road	北辰西路	Beichen West Road	2.6
惠新东街	Huixin East Street	惠新东桥	Huixin East Bridge	太阳宫路	Taiyanggong Road	1.3
惠新西街1	Huixin West Street 1	北四环	North 4th Ring Road	北土城东路	North Tucheng Road East	1.4
惠新西街2（北苑路支线一）	Huixin West Street 2 (Access Road One of Beiyuan Road)	慧忠路	Huizhong Road	北四环	North 4th Ring Road	0.7
建材城中路	Jiancaicheng Middle Road	五星啤酒厂	Wuxing Brewery	西小口路	Xixiaokou Road	1.7
建国路	Jianguo Road	大望桥	Dawangqiao	大北窑桥	Dabeiyaoqiao	1.4
建国门内大街	Jianguomen Inner Street	建国门桥	Jianguomenqiao	东单北大街	Dongdan North Street	1.5
建国门外大街	Jianguomen Outer Street	大北窑桥	Dabeiyaoqiao	建国门桥	Jianguomenqiao	2.3
姜庄路	Jiangzhuang Road	北湖渠西路（鼎城路）	Beihuqu West Road (Dingcheng Road)	南湖渠西路	Nanhuqu West Road	1.4
交道口东大街	Jiaodaokou East Street	北新桥路口	Beixinqiao Crossing	交道口路口	Jiaodaokou Crossing	0.7
金顶西街	Jinding West Street	金顶北路	Jinding North Road	金顶南路西口（阜石路）	Jinding South Road West Exit (Fushi Road)	0.6
金台路	Jintai Road	朝阳北路	Chaoyang North Road	朝阳路	Chaoyang Road	0.8
金榆路	Jinyu Road	机场第二高速	Airport Second Expressway	朝阳北路	Chaoyang North Road	10.2
金盏路	Jinzhan Road	机场第二高速	Airport Second Expressway	东苇路	Dongwei Road	2.4

3-5 （续表五）

路线名称	Route Name	起点名称	From	终点名称	To	通车里程（公里） Mileage (km)
劲松路	Jinsong Road	劲松桥	Jinsongqiao	光明桥	Guangmingqiao	1.4
京良路	Jingliang Road	京开路	Jingkai Road	优龙路	Youlong Road	5.4
京门新线	Jingmen New Line	京门公路与五里坨西一路交叉口	Intersection of Jingmen Highway and Wulitun West Road 1	京门新线2号桥东	Jingmen New Line No. 2 Bridge East	1.6
京顺路	Jingshun Road	孙河大桥北	Sunhe Bridge North	三元桥	Sanyuanqiao	14.0
静安西街	Jing'an West Street	北三环东路	North 3rd Ring East Road	七圣南路	Qisheng South Road	0.6
酒仙桥路	Jiuxianqiao Road	京顺路	Jingshun Road	东风南路	Dongfeng South Road	4.4
酒仙桥南路	Jiuxianqiao South Road	酒仙桥路	Jiuxianqiao Road	东四环路	East 4th Ring Road	0.9
开阳路	Kaiyang Road	开阳桥	Kaiyangqiao	万芳桥	Wanfangqiao	1.5
看丹南路	Kandan South Road	外环西路	Outer Ring West Road	榆树庄东路	Yushuzhuang East Road	2.0
康营东路	Kangying East Road	京平高速	Jingping Expressway	机场高速	Airport Expressway	1.4
科技大道	Keji Avenue	西四环南路	West 4th Ring South Road	丰草河	Fengcaohe	1.1
科荟路	Kehui Road	北苑路	Beiyuan Road	八达岭高速	Badaling Expressway	4.7
来广营西路	Laiguangying West Road	来广营南路	Laiguangying South Road	五环路	5th Ring Road	2.2
蓝靛厂北路河东	Landianchang North Road, Easton	火器营桥	Huoqiyingqiao	长春桥	Changchunqiao	2.1
蓝靛厂北路河西	Landianchang North Road, Weston	火器营桥	Huoqiyingqiao	长春桥（长春桥南深槽路段终点）	Changchunqiao (the end of Changchunqiao South Underpass)	2.2
蓝靛厂南路河东	Landianchang North Road, Easton	长春桥	Changchunqiao	西翠路北桥北伸缩缝	North Expansion Joint of Xicui Road North Bridge	4.5
蓝靛厂南路河西	Landianchang Sorth Road, Weston	长春桥（长春桥南深槽路段终点）	Changchunqiao (the end of Changchunqiao South Underpass)	翠微路口北（阜成路立交桥南深槽路段终点）	Cuiwei Crossing North (the end of Fucheng Road Flyover South Underpass)	3.8
丽泽路	Lize Road	菜户营桥	Caihuyingqiao	丽泽桥	Lizeqiao	3.0
亮马桥路	Liangmaqiao Road	东四环路	East 4th Ring Road	东三环路	East 3rd Ring Road	2.5
林萃路	Lincui Road	五环路	5th Ring Road	大屯路	Datun Road	2.3

3-5 （续表六）

路线名称 Route Name		起点名称 From		终点名称 To		通车里程 （公里） Mileage (km)
玲珑路	Linglong Road	花园桥	Huayuanqiao	西四环	West 4th Ring Road	3.1
榴乡路	Liuxiang Road	南三环	South 3rd Ring Road	虎殿路出口	Wudian Road Exit	3.0
鲁谷东路	Lugu East Road	石景山路	Shijingshan Road	八宝山南路	Babaoshan South Road	2.0
骡马市大街	Luomashi Street	虎坊桥	Hufangqiao	菜市口	Caishikou	0.9
马家堡东路	Majiapu East Road	陶然亭桥	Taorantingqiao	大红门西路	Dahongmen West Road	3.5
马家堡西路	Majiapu West Road	万芳桥	Wanfangqiao	南四环路	South 4th Ring Road	2.8
马连道北路	Maliandao North Road	广莲路	Guanglian Road	广安门外大街	Guang'anmen Outer Street	0.4
马连洼北路	Malianwa North Road	信息路	Xinxi Road	黑山扈路	Heishanhu Road	3.8
毛纺路	Maofang Road	小营西路	Xiaoying West Road	南滨河路	Nanbinhe Road	1.3
梅市口路	Meishikou Road	莲花池西路	Lianhuachi West Road	五环	5th Ring Road	5.8
南蜂窝路	Nanfengwo Road	莲花池东路	Lianhuachi East Road	广莲路	Guanglian Road	0.3
南马连道路	Nanmaliandao Road	广安门南滨河路	Guang'anmen-nanbinhe Road	莲花河	Lianhua River	0.6
南磨房路	Nanmofang Road	窑洼湖桥	Yaowahuqiao	劲松桥	Jinsongqiao	2.5
南新华街	Nanxinhua Street	宣武门东大街	Xuanwumen East Street	骡马市大街	Luomashi Street	1.2
南苑路	Nanyuan Road	木樨园桥	Muxiyuanqiao	警备东路	Jingbei East Road	6.0
牛街	Niujie Street	广安门内大街	Guang'anmen Inner Street	南横西街	Nanheng West Street	0.7
农展馆南路	Nongzhanguan South Road	朝阳公园西路	Chaoyang Park West Road	长虹桥	Changhongqiao	0.9
平安里西大街	Ping'anli West Street	西四北大街	Xisi North Street	官园桥	Guanyuanqiao	1.4
蒲黄榆路	Puhuangyu Road	玉蜓桥	Yutingqiao	刘家窑桥	Liujiayaoqiao	1.5
前门大街	Qianmen Street	前门箭环路	Qianmen Ring Road	永安路	Yongan Road	1.4
前门东大街	Qianmen East Street	台基厂大街	Taijichang Street	广场西侧路	Guangchang West Side Road	1.3
前门箭环路	Qianmen Ring Road	前门东大街	Qianmen East Street	前门西大街	Qianmen West Street	0.5
前门西大街	Qianmen West Street	人大东侧路	Renda East Side Road	宣武门东大街	Xuanwumen East Street	1.0

3-5 （续表七）

路线名称 Route Name		起点名称 From		终点名称 To		通车里程 （公里） Mileage (km)
青年路	Qingnian Road	平房新村北街	Pingfangxincun North Street	姚家园路	Yaojiayuan Road	2.7
清华东路	Tsinghua East Road	双清路	Shuangqing Road	八达岭高速	Badaling Expressway	2.8
人大东侧路	Renda East Side Road	西长安街	Xichang'an Street	前门西大街	Qianmen West Street	0.8
人大西侧路	Renda West Side Road	西长安街	Xichang'an Street	前门西大街	Qianmen West Street	1.0
人民大会堂南侧路	South Side Road of the Great Hall of the People	人民大会堂东侧路	East Side Road of the Great Hall of the People	人民大会堂西侧路	West Side Road of the Great Hall of the People	0.3
三里河东路	Sanlihe East Road	阜成门外大街	Fuchengmen Outer Street	复兴门外大街	Fuxingmen Outer Street	1.8
三里河路	Sanlihe Road	西外大街	Xiwai Street	复兴门外大街	Fuxingmen Outer Street	3.5
上地村西路	Shangdicun West Road	东北旺北路	Dongbeiwang North Road	西北旺南路	Xibeiwang South Road	1.2
上庄大街	Shangzhuang Street	阜石路	Fushi Road	石景山路	Shijingshan Road	2.1
石景山路	Shijingshan Road	玉泉路	Yuquan Road	北辛安路	Beixin'an Road	6.9
石榴庄路	Shiliuzhuang Road	成寿寺路	Chengshousi Road	南苑路	Nanyuan Road	3.9
石门路	Shimen Road	隆恩寺路（五里坨西路）	Longensi Road (Wulituo West Road)	金顶北路	Jinding North Road	4.6
手帕口北街	Shoupakou North Street	莲花池东路	Lianhuachi East Road	广安门外大街	Guang'anmen Outer Street	0.9
首体南路	Shouti South road	西直门外大街	Xizhimen Outer Street	阜成路	Fucheng Road	1.7
双龙路	Shuanglong Road	东四环（四方桥）	East 4th Ring Road (Sifangqiao)	西大望路	Xidawang Road	1.0
松榆南路	Songyu South Road	西大望路	Xidawang Road	东三环（华威桥）	East 3rd Ring Road (Huawei Bridge)	1.4
太平街	Taiping Street	北纬路	Beiwei Road	陶然亭桥	Taoranting Bridge	1.4
太平桥大街	Taipingqiao Street	白塔寺	Baitasi	复兴门内大街	Fuxingmen Inner Street	2.1
太阳宫南街	Taiyanggong South Street	太阳宫中路	Taiyanggong Middle Road	京承高速	Jingcheng Expressway	1.1
陶然亭路	Taoranting Road	太平街	Taiping Street	中央戏曲学院	Central Academy of Drama	1.6
体育馆路	Tiyuguan Road	左安门内大街	Zuo'anmen Inner Street	天坛东路	Tiantan East Road	1.2

3-5 (续表八)

路线名称 Route Name		起点名称 From		终点名称 To		通车里程 （公里） Mileage (km)
天桥南大街	Tianqiao South Street	永安路	Yongan Road	南纬路	Nanwei Road	0.6
天坛东路	Tiantan East Road	天坛路	Tiantan Road	玉蜓桥	Yutingqiao	1.8
甜水园街	Tianshuiyuan Street	朝阳公园南路	Chaoyang Park South Road	朝阳北路	Chaoyang North Road	1.2
万丰路	Wanfeng Road	莲花池西路	Lianhuachi West Road	丰台北路	Fengtai North Road	3.5
万寿路	Wanshou Road	阜成路立交桥南深槽路段终点	The end of Fucheng Road Flyover South Underpass	莲花池西路	Lianhuachi West Road	2.4
万寿路南延	South Extension of Wanshou Road	南四环路	South 4th Ring Road	金星路	Jinxing Road	7.6
望京北路	Wangjing North Road	溪阳东路	Xiyang East Road	南湖北路	Nanhu North Road	2.5
望京东路	Wangjing East Road	宏泰东街	Hongtai East Street	广顺南大街	Guangshun South Street	1.1
望京新干线	Wangjing Superexpress Line	宏泰东街	Hongtai East Street	阜通西大街	Futong West Street	0.4
魏公村路	Weigongcun Road	中关村南大街	Zhongguancun South Street	西三环北路	West 3rd Ring North Road	1.3
温阳路	Wenyang Road	沙阳路	Shayang Road	温北路	Wenbei Road	8.8
文津街	Wenjin Street	北长街	Beichang Street	府右街	Fuyou Street	0.8
五四大街	Wusi Street	美术馆东街	Meishuguan East Street	北池子大街	Beichizi Street	0.7
西长安街	Xichang'an Street	人大东侧路	Renda East Side Road	西单	Xidan	1.8
西大望路	Xidawang Road	朝阳路	Chaoyang Road	弘燕东路	Hongyan East Road	5.3
西单北大街	Xidan North Street	大酱房	Dajiangfang	西长安街	West Chang'an Street	1.3
西三旗东路	Xisanqi East Road	建材城西路	Jiancaicheng West Road	永泰庄北路	Yongtaizhuang North Road	2.7
西四北大街	Xisi North Street	地安门西大街	Di'anmen West Street	西四东大街	Xisi East Street	1.0
西四东大街	Xisi East Street	皇城根北街	Huangchenggen North Street	西四	Xisi	0.3
西四南大街	Xisi South Street	西四	Xisi	大酱坊	Dajiangfang	0.6
西直门内大街	Xizhimen Inner Street	新街口南大街	Xinjiekou South Street	西直门	Xizhimen	1.5
香河园路	Xiangheyuan Road	三元桥	Sanyuanqiao	东二环	East 2nd Ring Road	2.3

3-5 （续表九）

路线名称 Route Name		起点名称 From		终点名称 To		通车里程 （公里） Mileage (km)
霄云路	Xiaoyun Road	东四环路	East 4th Ring Road	三元东桥	Sanyuandongqiao	2.0
小屯路	Xiaotun Road	莲石路	Lianshi Road	京石辅路	Side road of Jingshi Expressway	3.6
小营东路	Xiaoying East Road	育慧北路	Yuhui North Road	小营路	Xiaoying Road	0.5
小营西路	Xiaoying West Road	小营路	Xiaoying Road	北苑路	Beiyuan Road	0.6
辛店村立交道路	Xindiancun Flyover Road	京承高速路东	Jingcheng Expressway East	新北路	Xinbei Road	0.5
辛店村路西延（石板房南路）	West Extension of Xindiancun Road (Shibanfang South Road)	八达岭高速	Badaling Expressway	学清路	Xueqing Road	0.8
新东路	Xindong Road	香河园路	Xiangheyuan Road	工人体育场北路	Workers Stadium North Road	2.2
新街口北大街	Xinjiekou North Street	积水潭桥	Jishuitanqiao	西直门内大街	Xizhimen Inner Street	0.9
新街口南大街	Xinjiekou South Street	西直门内大街	Xizhimen Inner Street	地安门西大街	Di'anmen West Street	0.9
新街口外大街	Xinjiekou Outer Street	北三环	North 3rd Ring Road	北二环	North 2nd Ring Road	2.1
新康路	Xinkang Road	德外大街	Dewai Street	新外大街	Xinwai Street	0.7
新永定门外大街	New Yongdingmen Outer Street	永定门桥	Yongdingmenqiao	木樨园桥	Muxiyuanqiao	1.7
信息路	Xinxi Road	西二旗南路（上地八街）	Xi'erqi South Road (Shangdi 8th Street)	清河（厢白旗桥）	Qinghe (Xiangbaiqi Bridge)	3.6
星火西路	Xinghuo West Road	酒仙桥路（东风南路）	Jiuxianqiao Road (Dongfeng South Road)	姚家园路	Yaojiayuan Road	2.0
杏石口路	Xingshikou Road	西四环	West 4th Ring Road	香山南路	Xiangshan South Road	5.6
宣武门东大街	Xuanwumen East Street	前门西大街	Qianmen West Street	宣武门西口	Xuanwumen West Exit	0.8
宣武门内大街	Xuanwumen Inner Street	复兴门内大街	Fuxingmen Inner Street	宣武门西大街	Xuanwumen West Street	0.8
宣武门外大街	Xuanwumen Outer Street	宣武门	Xuanwumen	菜市口大街	Caishikou Street	1.2
宣武门西大街	Xuanwumen West Street	宣武门内大街	Xuanwumen Inner Street	莲花池东路	Lianhuachi East Road	2.2

3-5 （续表十）

路线名称 Route Name		起点名称 From		终点名称 To		通车里程 （公里） Mileage (km)
学清路	Xueqing Road	昌平路（五环）	Changping Road (5th Ring Road)	清华东路	Tsinghua East Road	2.5
学院路（主干）	Xueyuan Road (Artery)	清华东路	Tsinghua East Road	北四环中路中	Center of North 4th Ring Middle Road	1.6
学院南路	Xueyuan South Road	新街口外大街	Xinjiekou Outer Street	中关村南大街	Zhongguancun South Street	4.1
姚家园新路	Yaojiayuan New Road	东坝中路	Dongba Middle Road	四环中	4th Ring Road Middle	5.1
颐和园路	Summer Palace Road	北四环路	North 4th Ring Road	香山路	Xiangshan Road	4.8
樱花园东街	Yinghuayuan East Street	太阳宫路	Taiyanggong Road	和平东桥	Hepingdongqiao	0.9
樱花园西街	Yinghuayuan West Street	太阳宫路	Taiyanggong Road	和平西桥	Hepingxiqiao	0.9
雍和宫大街	Yonghe Lama Temple Street	雍和宫桥	Yonghe Lama Temple Bridge	北新桥路口	Beixinqiao Crossing	0.9
永定门内大街	Yongdingmen Inner Street	南纬路	Nanwei Road	永定门桥	Yongdingmenqiao	1.1
右安门内大街	You'anmen Inner Street	南横西街	Nanheng West Street	右安门桥	You'anmenqiao	1.6
玉泉路	Yuquan Road	阜石路	Fushi Road	莲石东路	Lianshi East Road	3.1
育慧东路	Yuhui East Road	鼎成路	Dingcheng Road	育慧北路	Yuhui North Road	0.6
裕民中路	Yumin Middle Road	裕民路	Yumin Road	北三环中路	North 3rd Ring Middle Road	0.5
园博大道	Yuanbo Avenue	大灰厂东路	Daqingchang East Road	杜家坎环岛	Dujiakan Roundabout	6.6
园博园南路	Yuanboyuan South Road	五环	5th Ring Road	长兴路	Changxing Road	5.5
圆明园西路	Yuanmingyuan West Road	马连洼北路	Malianwa North Road	肖家河桥北伸缩缝	Xiaojiaheqiao North Expansion Joint	2.7
远大路	Yuanda Road	长春桥	Changchunqiao	西四环	West 4th Ring Road	1.6
皂君庙路	Zaojunmiao Road	北三环西路	North 3rd Ring West Road	学院南路	Xueyuan South Road	1.1
展览馆路	Zhanlanguan road	西外南街	Xiwai South Street	阜外大街	Fuwai Street	1.7
展西路	Zhanxi Road	高梁桥路	Gaoliangqiao Road	展览馆路	Zhanlanguan Road	2.2
张仪村路	Zhangyicun Road	吴家村路	Wujiacun Road	京石高速右辅路	Right Side Road of Jingshi Expressway	3.7
张自忠路	Zhang Zizhong Road	东四北大街	Dongsi North Street	美术馆后街	Meishuguan Back Street	0.7

3-5 （续表十一）

路线名称 Route Name		起点名称 From		终点名称 To		通车里程（公里）Mileage (km)
赵登禹路	Zhao Dengyu Road	西直门内大街	Xizhimen Inner Street	阜成门内大街	Fuchengmen Inner Street	1.9
知春路	Zhichun Road	学院路	Xueyuan Road	海淀南路	Haidian South Road	3.1
志新东路	Zhixin East Road	志新路	Zhixin Road	志新桥	Zhixinqiao	0.7
志新路	Zhixin Road	八达岭高速	Badaling Expressway	学院路	Xueyuan Road	2.2
中关村北大街	Zhongguancun North Street	体院西桥	Tiyuanxiqiao	北四环西路	North 4th Ring West Road	4.0
中关村大街	Zhongguancun Street	北四环西路	North 4th Ring West Road	北三环西路	North 3rd Ring West Road	2.1
中关村东路	Zhongguancun East Road	双清路	Shuangqing Road	北三环联想桥	North 3rd Ring Road Lianxiangqiao	3.1
中关村南大街	Zhongguancun South Street	北三环西路	North 3rd Ring West Road	西直门外大街	Xizhimen Outer Street	3.2
珠市口东大街	Zhushikou East Street	崇文门外大街	Chongwenmen Outer Street	前门大街	Qianmen Street	1.8
珠市口西大街	Zhushikou West Street	前门大街	Qianmen Street	虎坊桥	Hufangqiao	1.2
紫竹院路（主干）	Zizhuyuan Road (Artery)	紫竹院桥西	Zizhuyuanqiao West	四季青桥	Sijiqing Bridge	3.3
和平里北街	Hepingli North Street	柳芳北街	Liufang North Street	青年湖北街	Qingnianhu North Street	2.5
北苑东路	Beiyuan East Road	清河南侧滨河路	Qinghe South Binhe Road	北五环（外环）	North 5th Ring Road (outer ring)	4.4
东坝河中路	Dongbahe Middle Road	坝河北路	Bahe North Road	新姚家园路	Xinyaojiayuan Road	3.3
阜通西大街	Yutong West Street	阜安路	Fu'an Road	望京西路	Wangjing West Road	2.8
红军营南路	Hongjunying South Road	北苑东路	Beiyuan East Road	安立路	Anli Road	2.5
清苑路	Qingyuan Road	春华路	Chunhua Road	红军营南路	Hongjunying South Road	0.9
曙光西路	Shuguang West Road	北四环东路	North 4th Ring Road East	三元西桥	Sanyuanxiqiao	2.0
辛店路	Xindian Road	望京西路	Wangjing West Road	北苑路	Beiyuan Road	3.5
板井路	Banjing Road	车道沟桥	Chedaogouqiao	西四环	West 4th Ring Road	1.6
成府路	Chengfu Road	学院路	Xueyuan Road	中关村北大街	Zhongguancun North Street	3.2

3-5 （续表十二）

路线名称 Route Name		起点名称 From		终点名称 To		通车里程 （公里） Mileage (km)
旱河路	Hanhe Road	香泉环岛	Xiangquan Roundabout	阜石路	Fushi Road	8.2
黑泉路	Heiquan Road	西小口路	Xixiaokou Road	林萃桥	Lincuiqiao	4.2
巨山路	Jushan Road	杏石口路	Xingshikou Road	阜石路	Fushi Road	4.3
农大南路	Nongda South Road	信息路	Xinxi Road	圆明园西路	Yuanmingyuan West Road	2.7
前屯南路	Qiantun South Road	西三旗东路	Xisanqi East Road	前屯西路	Qiantun West Road	0.4
万安东路	Wan'an East Road	北坞村路	Beiwucun Road	旱河路	Hanhe Road	1.5
永丰路	Yongfeng Road	崔家窑路	Cuijiayao Road	北清路	Beiqing Road	6.4
玉泉山路	Yuquanshan Road	北坞村路	Beiwucun Road	香泉环岛	Xiangquan Roundabout	3.0
大灰厂路	Dahuichang Road	廊坡顶西	Langpoding West	云岗路	Yungang Road	10.7
南宫南路	Nangong South Road	大灰厂路	Dahuichang Road	铁匠营村北口（京石高速）	Tiejiangyingcun North Exit (Jingshi Expressway)	3.9
杨庄大街	Yangzhuang Street	苹果园南路	Pingguoyuan South Road	古城大街	Gucheng Street	1.1
东坝南二街	Dongba South 2th Street	机场第二高速辅路	Side Road of Airport Second Expressway	五环路（七棵树）	5th Ring Road(Qikeshu)	4.8
后厂村路	Houchangcun Road	西二旗桥	Xierqiqiao	永丰路	Yongfeng Road	4.1
立通路	Litong Road	小清河桥北伸缩缝	The North Side of Xiaoqingheqiao Expansion Joint	北苑路	Beiyuan Road	1.9
上地西路	Shangdi West Road	上地村西路	Shangdicun West Road	信息路	Xinxi Road	2.6
邓庄南路	Dengzhuang South Road	京包高速西侧辅路	West Side Road of Jingbao Expressway	永泽南路	Yongze South Road	3.0
广化大街	Guanghua Street	广渠路	Guangqu Road	化工路	Huagong Road	1.9
卢沟桥南路	Lugouqiao South Road	大瓦窑桥	Dawayaoqiao	杜家坎环岛	Dujiakan Roundabout	3.8
鲁坨路	Lutuo Road	鲁家山生物质能源厂	Lujiashan Biomass Energy Plant	羊圈头村	Yangjuantou Village	3.7
太阳宫路	Taiyanggong Road	太阳宫中路	Taiyanggong Middle Road	太阳宫北街	Taiyanggong North Street	0.3
西小口路	Xixiaokou Road	海淀区界	Haidian District Boundary	昌平路（左侧辅路）	Changping Road(Left Side Road)	2.7

3-5 （续表十三）

路线名称 Route Name	起点名称 From		终点名称 To		通车里程 （公里） Mileage (km)
二环路辅路 Side Road of 2nd Ring Road	-	-	-	-	32.7
三环路辅路 Side Road of 3rd Ring Road	-	-	-	-	48.3
四环路辅路 Side Road of 4th Ring Road	-	-	-	-	65.3
菜户营南路辅路 Side Road of Caihuying South Road	菜户营桥	Caihuyingqiao	京开路	Jingkai Road	2.1
京藏高速辅路 Side Road of Jingzang Expressway	西三旗桥北	Xisanqiqiao North	北三环中路	North 3rd Ring Middle Road	11.2
德胜门外大街辅路 Side Road of Deshengmen Outer Street	北三环	North 3rd Ring Road	北二环	North 2nd Ring Road	2.3
东北城角联络线辅路 Side Road of Dongbeichengjiao Contact Line	三环内环辅路	3rd Ring Road Inner Auxiliary Road	新东路	Xindong Road	1.1
丰台北路辅路 Side Road of Fengtai North Road	丽泽桥东	Lizeqiao East	四环路	4th Ring Road	2.8
丰体南路辅路 Side Road of Fengti South Road	四环路	4th Ring Road	京石高速	Jingshi Expressway	2.2
阜石路辅路 Side Road of Fushi Road	西四环辅路（外侧）	Side Road of West 4th Ring Road (outside)	双峪路	Shuangyu Road	15.2
机场二通道辅路 Side Road of Airport Channl Two	K000+000	K000+000	姚家园路左侧辅路	Left Side Road of Yaojiayuan Road	6.6
姚家园路辅路 Side Road of Yaojiayuan Road	管庄路（焦庄桥）	Guanzhuang Road (Jiaozhuangqiao)	平房桥西	Pingfangqiao West	6.1
机场高速辅路 Side Road of Airport Expressway	机场道口	Airport Crossing	大山子桥	Dashanziqiao	12.3
京承高速侧辅路 Side Road of Jingcheng Expressway	望和桥	Wangheqiao	北三环东路	North 3rd Ring Road East	2.8
京榆路辅路 Side Road of Jingyu Road	西马庄收费站	Ximazhuang Toll Gate	八里桥	Baliqiao	2.0
京开高速辅路 Side Road of Jingkai Expressway	玉泉营桥	Yuquanyingqiao	九龙山庄	Jiulongshanzhuang	4.9
京沈高速辅路 Side Road of Jingshen Expressway	辛庄路立交	Xinzhuang Road Flyover	四方桥	Sifangqiao	7.5
京港澳辅路 Side Road of Jinggang'ao Expressway	张仪村	Zhangyicun	西五环路	West 5th Ring Road	6.2

3-5 （续表十四）

路线名称 Route Name	起点名称 From	终点名称 To	通车里程 （公里） Mileage (km)
京通快速辅路	Side Road of Jingtong Rapid Road	京承立交	Jingcheng Flyover	大望桥西	Dawangqiao West	13.7
莲花池东路辅路	Side Road of Lianhuachi East Road	天宁寺桥	Tianningsiqiao	莲花桥	Lianhuaqiao	3.7
莲花池西路辅路	Side Road of Lianhuachi West Road	莲花桥西	Lianhuaqiao West	金家村桥西出口	Jinjiacunqiao West Exit	2.8
莲石东路辅路	Side Road of Lianshi East Road	西四环中路	West 4th Ring Middle Road	重型机械厂西路	Heavy Machinery Factory West Road	5.2
通惠河北路辅路	Side Road of Tonghuihe North Road	东四环	East 4th Ring Road	东二环	East 2nd Ring Road	4.5
万泉河路辅路	Side Road of Wanquanhe Road	颐和园路	Summer Palace Road	北三环西路	North 3rd Ring West Road	5.0
北五环（内环）辅路	Side Road of North 5th Ring Road(Inner Ring)	顾庄过街天桥	Guzhuang Overpass	八达岭辅路（水源九厂专用路）	Badaling Side Road (Special Road for Shuiyuan 9th Factory)	3.3
北五环（外环）辅路	Side Road of North 5th Ring Road(Outer Ring)	北苑东路	Beiyuan East Road	八达岭辅路（水源九厂专用路）	Badaling Side Road (Special Road for Shuiyuan 9th Factory)	3.7
五方立交辅路3	Side Road 3 of Wufang Flyover	王四营仓库	Wangsiying Warehouse	京沈北侧辅路	North Side Road of Jingshen Expressway	0.2
五方立交辅路4	Side Road 4 of Wufang Flyover	明渠	Mingqu Channel	京沈北侧辅路	North Side Road of Jingshen Expressway	0.2
五环路大羊坊立交辅路1	Side Road 1 of Dayangfang Flyover, 5th Ring Road	北京博展国际	Beijing Bozhan International	过街天桥	Overpass	0.5
五环路大羊坊立交辅路2	Side Road 2 of Dayangfang Flyover, 5th Ring Road	大羊坊路	Dayangfang Road	亦庄路口	Yizhuang Crossing	1.1
五环路大羊坊立交辅路3	Side Road 3 of Dayangfang Flyover, 5th Ring Road	大羊坊桥北侧	Dayangfangqiao North	大羊坊桥南侧	Dayangfangqiao South	0.1
五环平房立交道路1号辅路	Side Road 1 of Pingfang Flyover Road, 5th Ring Road	平房路	Pingfang Road	姚家园路	Yaojiayuan Road	0.5
五环平房立交道路2号辅路	Side Road 2 of Pingfang Flyover Road, 5th Ring Road	平房路	Pingfang Road	姚家园路	Yaojiayuan Road	0.3
五环平房立交道路3号辅路	Side Road 3 of Pingfang Flyover Road, 5th Ring Road	平房村	Pingfangcun	姚家园路	Yaojiayuan Road	0.02

3-5 （续表十五）

路线名称 Route Name	起点名称 From	终点名称 To	通车里程 （公里） Mileage (km)
五环平房立交道路4号辅路 Side Road 4 of Pingfang Flyover Road, 5th Ring Road	五环平房立交道路1号 Pingfang Flyover Road 1, 5th Ring Road	姚家园路 Yaojiayuan Road	0.1
西五环中路辅路 Side Road of West 5th Ring Middle Road	朝阳医院京西院区 Chaoyang Hospital Jingxi Campus	石景山路 Shijingshan Road	0.4
西土城路 Xitucheng Road	北土城西路 Beitucheng West Road	学院南路 Xueyuan South Road	2.1
土城西侧路 Tucheng West Side Road	知春路 Zhichun Road	学院南路 Xueyuan South Road	2.3
西直门北大街辅路 Side Road of Xizhimen North Street	明光桥 Mingguangqiao	西直门桥 Xizhimenqiao	1.6
西直门外大街辅路 Side Road of Xizhimen Outer Street	西直门桥 Xizhimenqiao	白石立交桥 Baishi Flyover	2.3
学院路辅路 Side Road of Xueyuan Road	清华东路 Tsinghua East Road	北土城西路 Beitucheng West Road	1.1
紫竹院路辅路 Side Road of Zizhuyuan Road	白石新桥 Baishixinqiao	紫竹院桥西 Zizhuyuanqiao West	1.4
京昆联络线辅路 Side Road of Jingkun Contact Line	左堤路 Zuodi Road	京石高速公路 Jingshi Expressway	8.9
西土城路 Xitucheng Road	北土城西路 Beitucheng West Road	学院南路 Xueyuan South Road	2.1
土城西侧路 Tucheng West Side Road	知春路 Zhichun Road	学院南路 Xueyuan South Road	2.3
西直门北大街辅路 Side Road of Xizhimen North Street	明光桥 Mingguangqiao	西直门桥 Xizhimenqiao	1.6
西直门外大街辅路 Side Road of Xizhimen Outer Street	西直门桥 Xizhimenqiao	白石立交桥 Baishi Flyover	2.3
学院路辅路 Side Road of Xueyuan Road	清华东路 Tsinghua East Road	北土城西路 Beitucheng West Road	1.1
紫竹院路辅路 Side Road of Zizhuyuan Road	白石新桥 Baishixinqiao	紫竹院桥西 Zizhuyuanqiao West	1.4
京昆联络线辅路 Side Road of Jingkun Contact Line	左堤路 Zuodi Road	京石高速公路 Jingshi Expressway	8.9

主要统计指标解释

城市道路里程：指报告期末，城市中供车辆、行人通行的，有交通功能的各种铺装道路和土路的实际长度。计量单位：公里。

统计范围：城市道路与公路以城市规划区的边线分界，以城市道路管理部门和公路管理部门的实际管理权限进行统计。

统计分组：按城市道路的功能分为：快速路、主干路、次干路、支路及以下。

快速路：指城市道路中设有中央分隔带，具有四条以上的车道，全部或部分采用立体交叉与控制出入，供车辆以较高的速度行驶的道路。

主干路：指在城市道路网中起骨架作用的道路。

次干路：指城市道路网中的区域性干路，与主干路相连接，构成完整的城市干路系统。

支路及以下城市道路包括：城市道路网中干路以外，联系次干路或供区域内部使用的道路；在城市范围内，全路或大部分地段两侧建有各式建筑物，设有人行道和各种市政公用设施的道路。

城市道路面积：指报告期末，城市中供车辆、行人通行的，有交通功能的各种铺装道路和土路的实际面积。计量单位：万平方米。

统计分组：同城市道路里程分组。

城市步道长度：指报告期末，城市中专供行人通行的，有交通功能的各种铺装道路和土路的实际长度。城市步道长度亦称为城市人行道长度。计量单位：公里。

统计分组：同城市道路里程分组。

城市步道面积：指报告期末，城市中专供行人通行的，有交通功能的各种铺装道路和土路的实际面积。城市步道面积亦称为城市人行道面积。计量单位：万平方米。

统计分组：同城市道路里程分组。

城市桥梁数量：指报告期末，城市道路中为跨越天然或人工障碍物而修建的构筑物数量，包括立交桥数量、跨河桥数量、跨铁路桥数量等。计量单位：座。

城市人行天桥数量：指报告期末，城市道路中为行人横穿车行道而修建的跨越道路的天桥数量。计量单位：座。

城市人行地道数量：指报告期末，城市道路中为行人横穿车行道而修建的穿越道路的地道数量。计量单位：处。

Explanatory Notes on Main Statistical Indicators

Length of urban road refers to the actual length of paved roads and unsurfaced road in the city for vehicles and pedestrians at the end of the report. Unit: km.

Statistical scope: Urban roads and highways are delimited by the boundary line of urban planning area, and counted according to the actual administrative authority of urban road administrative departments and highway administrative departments.

Statistical grouping: Divided into rapid road, trunk road, secondary trunk road, branch road and below by functions.

Rapid road refers to roads in which there is a central dividing strip with more than four lanes, all or part of which dimensional crossing structure and control access is used for vehicles to travel at a high speed.

Trunk road refers to the roads that plays the role of skeleton in the urban road network.

Secondary Trunk Road refers to the regional trunk road in the road network, which is connected with the trunk road to form a complete urban trunk road system.

Branch road and below include : Roads besides the trunk roads in the road network that connect secondary trunk roads or is for internal use within the region; Roads in urban areas where various buildings, pavements and municipal utilities are built on both sides.

Area of urban road refers to the actual area of paved roads and unsurfaced road in the city for vehicles and pedestrians at the end of the report. Unit: 10,000 sq. ms.

Statistical grouping: the same as length of urban road.

Length of urban footpath refers to the actual length of paved roads and unsurfaced roads in the city only for pedestrians at the end of the report. It is also known as the length of urban sidewalk. Unit: km.

Statistical grouping: the same as length of urban road. Unit: km.

Area of urban footpath refers to the actual area of paved roads and unsurfaced roads in the city only for pedestrians at the end of the report. It is also known as the area of urban sidewalk. Unit: 10 000 sq. ms.

Statistical grouping: The same as length of urban road.

Number of urban bridges refers to the number of structures built for crossing natural or man-made obstacles in urban roads at the end of the report, including the number of flyovers, river bridges and railway bridges. Unit: unit.

Number of urban pedestrian overcrossing refers to the number of overcrossing built for pedestrians to cross the roadway at the end of the report. Unit: unit.

Number of urban pedestrian underpass refers to the number of underpass built for pedestrians to cross the roadway at the end of a report. Unit: unit.

四、旅客运输
PASSENGER TRANSPORTATION

简 要 说 明
Brief Introduction

一、本篇资料反映北京市交通运输发展的基本情况，主要包括：轨道交通、公共电汽车、出租汽车、出租汽车省际客运、旅游客运、郊区客运、汽车租赁、机动车维修及汽车综合性能检测站情况。

二、北京市公路客运包括省际客运、旅游客运和郊区客运。

Ⅰ. Statistics in this chapter reflects the basic situation of transportation development of Beijing, mainly including rail transit, buses, interprovincial passenger transportation of taxies, tourist passenger transportation, suburban passenger transportation, vehicle rental, motor vehicle maintenance and synthetic vehicle performance test station, etc.

Ⅱ. Highway passenger transportation in Beijing includes interprovincial passenger transportation, tourist passenger transportation and suburban passenger transportation.

4-1 轨 道 交 通
Rail Transit

指标 Indicator		计量单位 Unit		数量 Number
运营车辆	Operating Vehicles	-	-	-
运营车数	Number of Operating Vehicles	辆	vehicle	5 628
标准运营车数	Number of Standard Operating Vehicles	标台	standard-vehicle	14 059
编组列数	Number of Columns	列	line	912
运营线路	Operating Routes	-	-	-
运营线路条数	Number of Operating Routes	条	route	22
运营线路总长度	Total length of Operating Routes	公里	km	637
运营服务	Operation Service	-	-	-
客运量	Passenger Traffic	万人次	10 000 person-times	384 843
旅客周转量	Turnover of Passenger Traffic	万人公里	10 000 person-kms	3 368 293
运营里程	Operating Length	万车公里	10 000 train-kms	59 672
从业人员	Employees	-	-	-
从业人员数	Number of Employees	人	person	40 164
其中：驾驶员人数	of which: Number of Drivers	人	person	5 697

4-2 轨道交通分线路运营情况
Operation of Rail Transit by Line

指标 Indicator	线路长度（公里）Line Length (km)	年客运总量（万人次）Annual Passenger Traffic (10 000 person-time)	早高峰时段进站量（万人次）Inbound Volume during Early Peak (10 000 person-time)	晚高峰时段进站量（万人次）Inbound Volume during Late Peak (10 000 person-time)	旅客周转量（万人公里）Turnover of Passenger Traffic (10 000 person-km)	日均客运量（万人次）Average Daily Passenger Traffic (10 000 person-time)	日均客运强度（万人次/公里）Average Daily Passenger Traffic Intensity (10 000 person-time/km)	日均平均运距（公里）Average Daily Transfer Distance (km)	高峰小时最大满载率（%）Maximum Load Factor of Peak Hour (%)	车站数（个）Number of Stations	换乘站 Transfer Station
合计 Total	636	384 843	161.2	133.3	3 368 293	1 054.4	1.7	16.5	–	391	59
1号线 Line 1	31	38 963	11.8	14.1	291 402	106.8	3.4	7.5	103.0	23	10
2号线 Line 2	23	32 824	8.5	13.9	166 658	89.9	3.9	5.1	69.0	18	10
4-大兴线 4-Daxing Line	50	45 113	15.8	14.2	424 921	123.6	2.5	9.4	126.0	35	10
5号线 Line 5	28	34 257	15.5	9.9	281 923	93.9	3.4	8.3	115.0	23	10
6号线 Line 6	53	31 268	15.5	11.2	328 073	85.7	2.0	10.4	124.0	32	10
7号线 Line 7	24	15 555	6.4	5.4	103 729	42.6	1.8	6.7	56.0	20	5
8号线 Line 8	31	13 968	7.6	3.8	128 978	38.3	1.3	9.2	98.0	19	6
8号线南段 Line 8 South	16	10	–	–	58	4.9	0.3	5.9	16.0	12	2
9号线 Line 9	17	18 710	5.0	5.2	116 189	51.3	3.0	6.2	124.0	13	7
10号线 Line 10	57	56 214	22.9	24.0	458 040	154.0	2.7	8.1	102.0	45	16
13号线 Line 13	41	24 306	12.0	8.2	261 909	66.6	1.6	10.8	121.0	16	8
14号线（西段）Line 14 (West Section)	12	2 236	1.7	0.5	12 182	6.1	0.5	5.5	58.0	7	2
14号线（东段）Line 14 (East Section)	32	21 336	7.1	8.4	167 521	58.5	1.8	7.9	103.0	21	8
15号线 Line 15	43	13 357	6.8	4.8	177 999	36.6	0.9	13.5	123.0	20	4
16号线（北段）Line 16 (North Section)	20	3 380	2.4	1.0	34 008	9.3	0.5	10.1	73.0	10	1
昌平线 Changping Line	31	8 372	6.1	2.1	113 980	22.9	0.7	13.7	132.0	12	2
房山线 Fangshan Line	25	5 184	3.9	0.8	78 025	14.2	0.6	15.0	123.0	12	2
亦庄线 Yizhuang Line	23	7 341	4.3	2.5	80 805	20.1	0.9	11.0	93.0	14	1
八通线 Batong Line	19	9 940	7.0	2.4	102 834	27.2	1.4	10.3	129.0	13	2
S1线 S1 Line	9	112	0.1	0.1	542	0.3	0.0	4.8	10.0	7	1
燕房线 Yanfang Line	14	600	0.3	0.1	4 656	1.6	0.1	7.8	31.0	9	1
机场线 Airport Line	28	1 228	0.3	0.6	29 901	3.4	0.1	24.4	108.0	4	2
西郊线 Xijiao Line	9	567	0.3	0.2	3 960	1.6	0.2	6.7	–	6	1

注：同一换乘站不重复计数。
Notice: No more repetition count on the same station.

4-3 前五位轨道交通站点及线路
Top 5 Rail Transit Stations and Lines

一、日均进站量前五位的轨道交通车站
Top 5 Rail Transit Stations in Terms of Average Daily Arrivals

排序 Sort	车站 Station		万人次 10 000 person-time
1	北京南站	Beijing South Railway Station	10
2	北京西站	Beijing West Railway Station	9
3	东直门	Dongzhimen	7
4	北京站	Beijing Railway Station	7
5	国贸	Guomao	6

二、日均换乘量前五位的轨道交通车站
Top 5 Rail Transit Stations in Terms of Average Daily Transfer Volume

排序 Sort	换乘站 Transfer Station		万人次 10 000 person-time
1	西直门	Xizhimen	23
2	宋家庄	Songjiazhuang	22
3	呼家楼	Hujialou	16
4	惠新西街南口	Huixin xijienankou	15
5	国家图书馆	National library	14

三、日均进站量前五位的轨道交通线路
Top 5 Rail Transit Lines in Terms of Average Daily Arrivals

排序 Sort	线路 Line		万人次 10 000 person-time
1	10号线	Line 10	84
2	4-大兴线	4- Daxing Line	66
3	1号线	Line 1	53
4	5号线	Line 5	47
5	2号线	Line 2	45

4-4 轨道交通运营线路换乘站
Transfer Station of Rail Transit Operating Lines

序号 No.	换乘站名称	Transfer Station	连接轨道交通运营线路	Operating Lines Connected
1	公主坟站	Gongzhufen Station	1号线、10号线之间	Between Line 1 and Line 10
2	军事博物馆站	Military Museum Station	1号线、9号线之间	Between Line 1 and Line 9
3	复兴门站	Fuxingmen Station	1号线、2号线之间	Between Line 1 and Line 2
4	西单站	Xidan Station	1号线、4号线之间	Between Line 1 and Line 4
5	东单站	Dongdan Station	1号线、5号线之间	Between Line 1 and Line 5
6	建国门站	Jianguomen Station	1号线、2号线之间	Between line 1 and Line 2
7	国贸站	Guomao Station	1号线、10号线之间	Between Line 1 and Line 10
8	四惠站	Sihui Station	1号线、八通线之间	Between Line 1 and Batong Line
9	四惠东站	Sihui East Station	1号线、八通线之间	Between Line 1 and Batong Line
10	西直门站	Xizhimen Station	2号线、4号线、13号线之间	Between Line 2, Line 4, Line 13
11	鼓楼大街站	Gulou Street Station	2号线、8号线之间	Between Line 2 and Line 8
12	雍和宫站	Yonghe Lama Temple Station	2号线、5号线之间	Between Line 2 and Line 5
13	东直门站	Dongzhimen Station	2号线、13号线、机场线之间	Between Line 2, Line 13, Airport Line
14	朝阳门站	Chaoyangmen Station	2号线、6号线之间	Between Line 2 and Line 6
15	崇文门站	Chongwenmen Station	2号线、5号线之间	Between Line 2 and Line 5
16	宣武门站	Xuanwumen Station	2号线、4号线之间	Between Line 2 and Line 4
17	车公庄站	Chegongzhuang Station	2号线、6号线之间	Between Line 2 and Line 6
18	海淀黄庄站	Haidian Huangzhuang Station	10号线、4号线之间	Between Line 10 and Line 4
19	知春路站	Zhichun Road Station	10号线、13号线之间	Between Line 10 and Line 13
20	北土城站	Beitucheng Station	10号线、8号线之间	Between Line 10 and Line 8
21	惠新西街南口站	Huixin xijienankou Station	10号线、5号线之间	Between Line 10 and Line 5
22	芍药居站	Shaoyaoju Station	10号线、13号线之间	Between Line 10 and Line 13
23	三元桥站	Sanyuanqiao Station	10号线、机场线之间	Between Line 10 and Airport Line
24	呼家楼站	Hujialou Station	10号线、6号线之间	Between Line 10 and Line 6
25	宋家庄站	Songjiazhuang Station	10号线、5号线、亦庄线之间	Between Line 10, Line 5 and Yizhuang Line
26	角门西站	Jiaomen West Station	10号线、4号线之间	Between Line 10 and Line 4
27	西局站	Xiju Station	10号线、14号线之间	Between Line 10 and Line 14
28	六里桥站	Liuliqiao Station	10号线、9号线之间	Between Line 10 and Line 9
29	慈寿寺站	Cishousi Station	10号线、6号线之间	Between Line 10 and Line 6
30	西二旗站	Xierqi Station	13号线、昌平线之间	Between Line 13 and Changping Line

4-4（续表一）

序号 No.	换乘站名称	Transfer Station	连接轨道交通运营线路	Operating Lines Connected
31	霍营站	Huoying Station	13号线、8号线之间	Between Line 13 and Line 8
32	立水桥站	Lishuiqiao Station	13号线、5号线之间	Between Line 13 and Line 5
33	望京西站	Wangjing West Railway Station	13号线、15号线之间	Between Line 13 and Line 15
34	郭公庄站	Guogongzhuang Station	9号线、房山线之间	Between Line 9 and Fangshan Line
35	七里庄站	Qilizhuang Station	9号线、14号线之间	Between Line 9 and Line 14
36	北京西站站	Beijing West Railway Station	9号线、7号线之间	Between Line 9 and Line 7
37	白石桥南站	Baishiqiao South Station	9号线、6号线之间	Between Line 9 and Line 6
38	国家图书馆站	National Library Station	9号线、4号线之间	Between Line 9 and Line 4
39	平安里站	Ping'anli Station	6号线、4号线之间	Between Line 6 and Line 4
40	南锣鼓巷站	Nanluoguxiang Station	6号线、8号线之间	Between Line 6 and Line 8
41	东四站	Dongsi Station	6号线、5号线之间	Between Line 6 and Line 5
42	金台路站	Jintailu Station	6号线、14号线之间	Between Line 6 and Line 14
43	菜市口站	Caishikou Station	7号线、4号线之间	Between Line 7 and Line 4
44	磁器口站	Ciqikou Station	7号线、5号线之间	Between Line 7 and Line 5
45	奥林匹克公园站	Olympic Green Station	8号线、15号线之间	Between Line 8 and Line 15
46	朱辛庄站	Zhuxinzhuang Station	8号线、昌平线之间	Between Line 8 and Changping Line
47	望京站	Wangjing Station	14号线、15号线之间	Between Line 14 and Line 15
48	大望路站	Dawanglu Station	14号线、1号线之间	Between Line 14 and Line 1
49	九龙山站	Jiulongshan Station	14号线、7号线之间	Between Line 14 and Line 7
50	十里河站	Shilihe Station	14号线、10号线之间	Between Line 14 and Line 10
51	蒲黄榆站	Puhuangyu Station	14号线、5号线之间	Between Line 14 and Line 5
52	北京南站站	Beijing South Railway Station	14号线、4号线之间	Between Line 14 and Line 4
53	大屯路东站	Datun Road East Station	15号线、5号线之间	Between Line 15 and Line 5
54	西苑站	Xiyuan Station	16号线、4号线之间	Between Line 16 and Line 4
55	巴沟站	Bagou Station	10号线、西郊线	Between Line 10 and Xijiao Line
56	阎村东站	Yancun East Station	燕房线、房山线	Between Yanfang Line and Fangshan Line
57	珠市口站	Zhushikou Station	7号线、8号线南段	Between Line 7 and Line 8 South
58	永定门外站	Yongdingmenwai Station	14号线东段、8号线南段	Between Line 14 East and Line 8 South
59	金安桥站	Jinanqiao Station	S1线、6号线	Between Line S1 and Line 6

4-5 公共电汽车
Public Trolley Buses

指标 Indicator		计量单位 Unit	数量 Number
运营车辆	Operating Vehicles	–	–
运营车数	Number of Operating Vehicles	辆 vehicle	24 076
其中：空调车	of which: Air-conditioned Vehicle	辆 vehicle	22 500
其中：安装卫星定位车载终端的车辆	of which: Equipped with Satellite Positioning Vehicle Terminals	辆 vehicle	24 076
其中：BRT 运营车辆	of which: BRT Operating Vehicles	辆 vehicle	362
运营车数按车长分：	By Vehicle Length:	–	–
≤ 5 米	≤ 5 meters	辆 vehicle	–
> 5 米且 ≤ 7 米	>5 meters and ≤ 7 meters	辆 vehicle	402
> 7 米且 ≤ 10 米	>7 meters and ≤ 10 meters	辆 vehicle	511
> 10 米且 ≤ 13 米	>10 meters and ≤ 13 meters	辆 vehicle	16 983
> 13 米且 ≤ 16 米	>13 meters and ≤ 16 meters	辆 vehicle	3 625
> 16 米且 ≤ 18 米	>16 meters and ≤ 18 meters	辆 vehicle	928
> 18 米	>18 meters	辆 vehicle	–
双层车	Double Decker	辆 vehicle	1 627
运营车数按燃料类型分：	By Type of Fuel	–	–
汽油车	Gasoline Vehicle	辆 vehicle	
乙醇汽油车	Ethanol Gasoline Vehicle	辆 vehicle	
柴油车	Diesel Vehicle	辆 vehicle	7 982
液化石油气车	Liquefied Petroleum Gas Vehicle	辆 vehicle	–
天然气车	Natural Gas Vehicle	辆 vehicle	8 583
双燃料车	Dual Fuel Vehicle	辆 vehicle	–
无轨电车	Trolleybus	辆 vehicle	1 326
纯电动车	BEV	辆 vehicle	5 318
混合动力车	Hybrid Vehicle	辆 vehicle	862
其他	Others	辆 vehicle	5

4-5 （续表一）

指标 Indicator		计量单位 Unit		数量 Number
运营车数按排放标准分：	By Emission Standards:	—	—	—
国Ⅲ及以下	National Grade Ⅲ and below	辆	vehicle	193
国Ⅳ	National Grade Ⅳ	辆	vehicle	6 836
国Ⅴ及以上	National Grade Ⅴ and above	辆	vehicle	10 398
零排放	Zero Emission	辆	vehicle	6 649
标准运营车数	Standard Operating Vehicle	标台	standard-vehicle	33 980
本年新增运营车数	New Vehicles into Operation this Year	辆	vehicle	—
本年报废更新运营车数	Scrapped Vehicles Updated this Year	辆	vehicle	3 530
额定载客量	Rated Passenger Capacity	人	person	2 194 585
场站设施	**Station Facilities**	—	—	—
公交调度指挥中心	Public Transportation Dispatch and Command Center	个	pc	1
停车保养场面积	Parking Area	平方米	sq. m	5 824 511
运营线路	**Operation Lines**	—	—	—
运营线路条数	Number of Operation Lines	条	line	888
运营线路总长度	Total Length of Operation Line	公里	km	19 245
其中：BRT 线路长度	of which: BRT Line Length	公里	km	102
无轨电车线路长度	Trolley Bus Line Length	公里	km	433
运营服务	**Operation Service**	—	—	—
客运量	Passenger Traffic	万人次	10 000 person-time	318 975
其中：BRT 客运量	of which: BRT Passenger Traffic	万人次	10 000 person-time	4 760
其中：使用 IC 卡的客运量	of which: Passengers Using IC Cards	万人次	10 000 person-time	213 383
运营里程	Operating Length	万公里	10 000 km	126 880
从业人员	**Employees**	—	—	—
从业人员数	Number of Employees	人	person	85 763

4-6 出租汽车
Taxi

指标 Indicator		计量单位 Unit		数量 Number
运营车辆	Operating Vehicles	–	–	–
运营车数	Number of Operating Vehicles	辆	vehicle	70 035
其中：个体车辆	of which: Individual Vehicles	辆	vehicle	1 164
其中：安装卫星定位车载终端的车辆	of which: Equipped with Satellite Positioning Vehicle Terminals	辆	vehicle	70 035
运营车数按燃料类型分：	By Type of Fuel	–	–	–
汽油车	Gasoline Vehicles	辆	vehicle	65 009
双燃料车	Dual Fuel Vehicle	辆	vehicle	1 144
纯电动车	BEV	辆	vehicle	1 047
其他	Others	辆	vehicle	2 835
本年新增运营车数	New Operating Vehicles in this Year	辆	vehicle	1 551
本年报废更新运营车数	Scrapped Vehicles Updated in this Year	辆	vehicle	3 770
运营服务	Operation Service	–	–	–
载客车次总数	Total Number of Passenger Trips	万车次	10 000 vehicle-time	24 301
客运量	Passenger Traffic	万人次	10 000 person-time	34 021
运营里程	Operating Length	万公里	10 000 km	438 870
其中：载客里程	of which: Passenger Transportation Length	万公里	10 000 km	281 000
从业人员	Employees	–	–	–
从业人员数	Number of Employees	人	person	84 853

4-7 省际客运
Interprovincial Passenger Transportation

指标 Indicator		计量单位 Unit		数量 Number
基础设施	Infrastructure	—	—	—
等级客运站	Graded Passenger Station	个	unit	8
其中：一级站	of which: First-grade Station	个	unit	5
二级站	Second-grade Station	个	unit	3
其中：客运枢纽	of which: Passenger Transportation Hub	个	unit	1
运营线路	Operating Route	—	—	—
运营线路条数	Number of Operating Routes	条	route	737
运营线路长度	Length of Operating Routes	公里	km	372 185
运输服务	Transportation Service	—	—	—
客运量	Passenger Traffic	万人次	10 000 person-time	1 447
到达量	Arrival Passenger Number	万人次	10 000 person-time	744
发送量	Dispatched Passenger Number	万人次	10 000 person-time	702
旅客周转量	Turnover of Passenger Traffic	万人公里	10 000 person-km	504 447
平均日发班次	Average Daily Dispatched Runs	班次/日	run/day	1 280
其中：一级站	of which: First-grade Station	班次/日	run/day	1 054
二级站	Second-grade Station	班次/日	run/day	226
平均日旅客发送量	Average Daily Dispatched Passenger Number	人次	person-time	19 245
其中：一级站	of which: First-grade Station	人次	person-time	15 516
二级站	Second-grade Station	人次	person-time	3 729
经营从业人员	Operators and Employees	人	person	932

注：本表为省际客运站运营数据。
Notice: This table is the operation data of interprovincial passenger stations.

4-8 旅游客运
Tourist Passenger Transportation

指标 Indicator		计量单位 Unit		数量 Number
车辆数量	Number of Vehicle	辆	vehicle	6 592
		客位	seat	257 479
按标记客位分	By Rated Seat	—	—	—
大型	Large-size	辆	vehicle	4 814
		客位	seat	232 307
中型	Medium-size	辆	vehicle	887
		客位	seat	17 841
小型	Small-size	辆	vehicle	891
		客位	seat	7 331
按燃料类型分	By Type of Fuel	—	—	—
柴油车	Diesel Vehicle	辆	vehicle	4 751
汽油车	Gasoline Vehicle	辆	vehicle	1 399
电车	Battery Electric Vehicle	辆	vehicle	343
天然气车	Natural Gas Vehicle	辆	vehicle	99
其他	Others	辆	vehicle	—
运营服务	Operation Service	—	—	—
客运量	Passenger Traffic	万人次	10,000 person-time	4 129
旅客周转量	Turnover of Passenger Traffic	万人公里	10,000 person-km	319 327
经营业户数	Number of Business Operators	个	unit	76
100 辆及以上	100 vehicles and above	个	unit	12
50~99 辆	50-99 vehicles	个	unit	8
10~49 辆	10-49 vehicles	个	unit	31
5~9 辆	5-9 vehicles	个	unit	8
5 辆以下	5 vehicles and below	个	unit	17
从业人员数	Number of Employees	人	person	8 520

4-9 郊区客运
Suburban Passenger Transportation

指标 Indicator		计量单位 Unit		数量 Number
车辆数量	Number of Vehicle	辆	vehicle	5 046
		客位	seat	202 258
按燃料类型分	By Type of Fuel	-	-	-
汽油车	Gasoline Vehicle	辆	vehicle	1
柴油车	Diesel Vehicle	辆	vehicle	873
天然气车	Natural Gas Vehicle	辆	vehicle	973
双燃料车	Dual-fuel Vehicle	辆	vehicle	-
纯电动车	Battery Electric Vehicle	辆	vehicle	2 789
混合动力车	Hybrid Vehicle	辆	vehicle	410
其他燃料车	Others	辆	vehicle	-
郊区客运站数量	Number of Suburban Passenger Station	个	unit	191
运营线路	Operating Route	-	-	-
运营线路条数	Number of Operating Routes	条	route	430
运营线路总长度	Length of Operating Routes	公里	km	16 290
运营服务	Operation Service	-	-	-
客运量	Passenger Traffic	万人次	10,000 person-time	39 620
旅客周转量	Turnover of Passenger Traffic	万人公里	10,000 person-km	495 085
经营业户数	Number of Business Operators	户	unit	14
从业人员数	Number of Employees	人	person	8 708

4-10 公路营运载
Possession of Commercial

		计量单位 Unit	计量单位 Unit	总计 Total	按标记客位分 By Rated Seat		
					大型 Large-size	中型 Medium-size	小型 Mini-size
合 计	Total	辆	vehicle	75 262	8 903	2 668	63 691
		客位	seat	826 620	425 241	61 208	340 171
其中：卧铺客车	of which: Sleeper Coach	辆	vehicle	257	254	3	—
		客位	seat	9 646	9 561	85	—
按经营范围分	By Business Scope	—	—	—	—	—	—
班车客运客车	Shuttle Bus	辆	vehicle	824	792	32	
		客位	seat	34 043	33 215	828	—
旅游客车	Touring Bus	辆	vehicle	6 592	4 814	887	891
		客位	seat	257 479	232 307	17 841	7 331
其他客车	Others	辆	vehicle	67 846	3 297	1 749	62 800
		客位	seat	535 098	159 719	42 539	332 840
按燃料类型分	By Type of Fuel	—	—	—	—	—	—
汽油车	Gasoline Vehicle	辆	vehicle	49 200	—	—	—
柴油车	Diesel Vehicle	辆	vehicle	6 411	—	—	—
天然气车	Natural Gas Vehicle	辆	vehicle	1 109	—	—	—
纯电动车	Battery Electric Vehicle	辆	vehicle	18 132	—	—	—
混合动力车	Hybrid Vehicle	辆	vehicle	410			

客汽车拥有量
Highway Passenger Vehicles

按车长分 By Vehicle Length				按等级分 By Class			安装卫星定位车载终端 Equipped with Satellite Positioning Vehicle Terminals
特大型 Extra Large-size	大型 Large-size	中型 Medium-size	小型 Mini-size	高级 High Class	中级 Middle Class	普通 Ordinary Class	
123	7 696	3 568	63 875	4 631	64 515	6 116	75 262
5 327	377 745	98 752	344 796	230 822	384 175	211 623	826 620
97	160	—	—	257	—	—	257
3 753	5 893	—	—	9 646	—	—	9 646
—	—	—	—	—	—	—	—
122	576	126	—	821	3	—	824
5 274	24 302	4 467	—	33 928	115	—	34 043
1	3 823	1 693	1 075	3 810	1 712	1070	6 592
53	193 724	51 746	11 956	196 894	51 220	9 365	257 479
—	3 297	1 749	62 800	—	62 800	5 046	67 846
—	159 719	42 539	332 840	—	332 840	202 258	535 098
—	—	—	—	—	—	—	—
—	—	—	—	—	—	—	—
—	—	—	—	—	—	—	—
—	—	—	—	—	—	—	—
—	—	—	—	—	—	—	—

4-11 汽车租赁
Vehicle Rental

指标 Indicator		计量单位 Unit		数量 Number
租赁车辆数量	Number of Leased Vehicles	辆	vehicle	62 800
按客位数分	By Passenger Seat Number	–	–	–
5 座及以下的客车	5 seats and less	辆	vehicle	56 570
6~9 座的客车	6~9 seats	辆	vehicle	6 230
10 座以上的客车	10 seats and above	辆	vehicle	–
按燃料类型分	By Type of Fuel	辆	vehicle	
汽油车	Gasoline Vehicle	辆	vehicle	47 800
纯电动车	Battery Electric Vehicle	辆	vehicle	15 000
天然气车	Natural Gas Vehicle	辆	vehicle	–
经营业户数	Number of Business Operators	户	unit	627
10 辆以下	10 vehicles and below	户	unit	278
10~49 辆	10~49 vehicles	户	unit	205
50~100 辆	50~100 vehicles	户	unit	60
101~300 辆	101~300 vehicles	户	unit	45
301~999 辆	301~999 vehicles	户	unit	28
1000 辆及以上	1000 vehicles and above	户	unit	11
从业人员数	Number of Employees	人	person	8700
汽车租赁率	Car Rental Rate	%	%	80

4-12 机动车维修业及汽车综合性能检测站
Motor Vehicle Maintenance and Synthetic Vehicle Performance Test Station

指标 Indicator		计量单位 Unit		数量 Number
机动车维修业	Motor vehicle maintenance	-	-	-
经营业户	Number of Business Operators	户	unit	3 760
其中：汽车维修	of which: Auto Maintenance	户	unit	3 751
内：一类汽车维修	including: Class Ⅰ Auto Maintenance	户	unit	805
二类汽车维修	Class Ⅱ Auto Maintenance	户	unit	1 521
三类汽车维修	Class Ⅲ Auto Maintenance	户	unit	1 425
摩托车维修	Motorcycle Maintenance	户	unit	9
完成主要工作量	Main Workload	辆（台）次	vehicle-time	10 773 601
其中：整车修理	of which: Complete Vehicle Repair	辆次	vehicle-time	5 018
总成修理	Unit Repair	台次	vehicle-time	10 148
二级维护	Second Maintenance	辆次	vehicle-time	518 586
专项修理	Special Repair	辆次	vehicle-time	10 127 522
维修救援	Service Rescue	辆次	vehicle-time	112 327
从业人员数	Number of Employees	人	person	69 696
其中：技术负责人	of which: Technical Director	人	person	3 760
质量检验员	Quality Inspector	人	person	9 834
其他维修技术人员	Other Maintenance Technicians	人	person	31 795
汽车综合性能检测站	Synthetic Vehicle Performance Test Station	-	-	-
检测站	Test Stations	个	unit	11
完成检测量	Total Test Amount	辆次	vehicle-time	171 369
其中：维修竣工检测	of which: Maintenance Completion Test	辆次	vehicle-time	3 400
等级评定检测	Rating Test	辆次	vehicle-time	167 935
维修质量监督检测	Maintenance Quality Supervision Test	辆次	vehicle-time	34
其他检测	Other Tests	辆次	vehicle-time	-
内：排放检测	including: Emission test	辆次	vehicle-time	-
从业人员数	Number of Employees	人	person	282

主要统计指标解释

轨道交通车站数：指报告期末，轨道交通运营线路上供乘客候车和上下车的场所个数。计量单位：个。

轨道交通换乘站数：指报告期末，轨道交通运营线路上，乘客能从同一站台或通过专用通道从一条轨道交通线路转乘其他轨道交通线路的车站数。计量单位：个。

计算方法：不同轨道交通线路换乘的站点按一个换乘站统计。

轨道交通运营线路条数：指报告期末，为轨道交通运营列车设置的固定线路总条数。计量单位：条。

计算方法：按规划设计为同一条线路但分期建成的线路，统计时仍按一条线路计算。

统计分组：一般包括地铁、轻轨、单轨、有轨电车、磁悬浮列车等。

轨道交通运营线路总长度：指报告期末，轨道交通全部运营线路长度之和。包括地面、地下、高架等线路，不包括折返、试车、联络线等非运营线路。计量单位：公里。

统计分组：同轨道交通运营线路条数分组。

轨道交通运营车数：指报告期末，城市用于轨道交通运营业务的全部车辆数。计量单位：辆。

计算方法：以企业（单位）固定资产台账中已投入运营的车辆数为准；新购、新制和调入的运营车辆，自投入之日起开始计算；调出、报废和调作他用的运营车辆，自上级主管机关批准之日起不再计入。地铁、轻轨、单轨和磁悬浮列车在统计时，一自然节统计为一辆，不按编组列统计。轨道交通系统的分类界定方法参照《城市公共交通分类标准》（CJJ/T 114—2007）执行。

轨道交通标准运营车数：指报告期末，不同类型的轨道交通运营车辆按统一的标准当量折算合成的运营车数。计量单位：标台。

计算公式：轨道交通标准运营车数（标台）= Σ（每类型车辆数 × 相应换算系数）。

轨道交通编组列数：指报告期末，辖区内已开通运营的各条轨道交通运营线路编组的列车数量合计数。计量单位：列。

轨道交通额定载客量：指报告期末，所有轨道交通运营车辆的核定载客人数之和。计量单位：人。

轨道交通高峰小时最大满载率：也称高峰时段最大断面满载率，指高峰时段轨道交通运营线路单向最大断面客流量与相应断面运力的比值。计量单位：%。

轨道交通客运量：指报告期内，轨道交通运送乘客的总人次，包括付费乘客和不付费乘客人次。计量单位：万人次。

轨道交通旅客周转量：指报告期内，轨道交通运送的每位乘客与其相应运送距离的乘积之和。计量单位：万人公里。

轨道交通日均客运量：指报告期内，轨道交通平均每日运送乘客的人次。计量单位：万人次。

公共电汽车运营车数：指报告期末，城市（县城）用于公共客运交通运营业务的全部公共电汽车车辆数。计量单位：辆。

计算方法：新购、新制和调入的运营车辆，自投入之日起开始计算；调出、报废和调作他用的运营车辆，自上级主管机关批准之日起不再计入。可按不同车长、不同燃料类型、不同排放标准和是否配备空调等分别统计。

统计分组：一般按以下方式分组：

（1）按车长分。如可分为≤5米、>5米且≤7米、>7米且≤10米、>10米且≤13米、>13米且≤16米、>16米且≤18米、>18米、双层车。

（2）按车辆燃料类型分。如可分为汽油车、乙醇汽油车、柴油车、液化石油气车、天然气车、双燃料车、无轨电车、纯电动车、混合动力车和其他燃料车。

（3）按排放标准分。如可分为国Ⅱ及以下、国Ⅲ、国Ⅳ、国Ⅴ及以上、零排放。

（4）按行驶区域分。如可分为市区公交车和市郊公交车。

公共电汽车标准运营车数：指报告期末，不同类型的公交运营车辆按统一的标准当量折算合成的运营车数。计量单位：标台。

计算公式：标准运营车数（标台）= Σ（每类型车辆数 × 相应换算系数）。

公共电汽车额定载客量：指报告期末，所有公共电汽车运营车辆核定载客人数之和。额定载客量亦称核定载客人数。计量单位：人。

计算公式：公共电汽车额定载客量 = 车厢固定乘客座位数 + 车厢有效站立面积（平方米）× 每平方米允许站立人数。

公共电汽车运营里程：指报告期内，公共电汽车运营车辆为运营而出车行驶的全部里程。计量单位：公里。

统计范围：公共电汽车运营里程包括载客里程和空驶里程，不包括为进行保养、修理而进出保修厂及试车的里程。其中载客里程指运营车辆载运乘客行驶的里程，包括运营车辆为运送乘客在线路行驶的里程和包车载客里程；空驶里程指运营车辆为运营规定而不载运乘客的空车行驶里程，包括从车场至线路出、回场里程，中途故障和其他原因空驶到起点、终点或车场的里程，包括回程的空驶里程。

出租汽车运营车数：指报告期末，已经领取出租汽车专用牌照的运营车辆数量，包括情况完好的、在修的、长期行驶的以及拟报废尚未经上级机关批准的车辆数量。计量单位：辆。

统计范围：出租汽车一般应符合以下要求：车辆技术性能、设施完好，车容整洁；出租汽车应当装置由客运管理机构批准的、并经技术监督部门鉴定合格的计价器；出租小客车应当装置经公安机关鉴定合格的防劫安全设施；出租汽车应当固定装置统一的顶灯和显示空车待租的明显标志。个体出租车指具有出租汽车专用牌照和营运证，经营性质为个体的出租汽车。

统计分组：一般按以下方式分组：

（1）按车辆燃料类型分。如可分为：汽油车、乙醇汽油车、柴油车、液化石油气车、天然气车、双燃料车、纯电动车、其他燃料车。

（2）按车辆运营方式分。如可分为：个体出租车和非个体出租车。

出租汽车运营里程：指报告期内，出租汽车客运运营车辆为运营而出车行驶的全部里程。包括载客里程和空驶里程。计量单位：万公里。

出租汽车载客里程：指报告期内，出租汽车客运运营车辆按照乘客意愿提供客运服务行驶计费的里程。计量单位：万公里。

计算公式：出租汽车载客里程＝里程表下客时数码－里程表上客时数码。

公共电汽车客运量：指报告期内，公共电汽车运送乘客的总人次，包括付费乘客和不付费乘客人次。计量单位：万人次。

出租汽车客运量：指报告期内，出租汽车运送乘客的总人次。计量单位：万人次。

计算公式：客运量＝载客车次总数×载客人数系数。

对于载客人数系数，各企业可根据掌握的实际客流调查资料进行确定，若无相关调查资料，按照平均每车次载客2人计。

公共电汽车运营线路条数：指报告期末，为公交运营车辆设置的固定运营线路条数。计量单位：条。

统计范围：公共电汽车运营线路条数包括干线、支线、专线和高峰时间行驶的固定线路条数，不包括临时行驶和联营线路条数。

统计分组：一般按以下方式分组：

（1）按区域分为：市区公交线路条数和市郊公交线路条数。

（2）按票制分为：分段计价票制运营线路条数和单一票制运营线路条数。

公共电汽车运营线路总长度：指报告期末，全部公共电汽车运营线路长度之和。计量单位：公里。

统计范围：公共电汽车运营线路长度不包括折返、试车、联络线等非运营线路的长度。

公共电汽车从业人员数：指报告期末，在公共电汽车经营业户中工作并取得劳动报酬的实有人员数量。计量单位：人。

统计分组：一般按从业人员所在的工作岗位进行分组。如驾驶员人数、售票员人数、乘务员人数等。

出租汽车从业人员数：指报告期末，在出租汽车经营业户中工作并取得劳动报酬的实有人员数量。计量单位：人。

统计分组：一般按从业人员所在的工作岗位进行分组。如驾驶员人数、财务人员数等。

客运站数量：指报告期末，经交通运输管理机构核定并取得经营许可的客运站数量。计量单位：个。

客运站数量按站级统计，站级划分按部颁标准《汽车客运站级别划分和建设要求》（JT/T 200—2004）执行。

统计分组：按客运站的等级分为：一级站、二级站、三级站、四级站、五级站、简易站及招呼站。

客运枢纽：指包含多种交通客运方式，能实现无缝换乘，具有运输组织管理、中转换乘、多式联运、通信信息和生产生活辅助服务等一项或多项基本功能的交通系统。计量单位：个。

客运枢纽是多种客运交通方式线路汇集的大型客流集散点。枢纽站中不同交通方式的场站设施实体建筑应在同一空间内布设或有专用通道相连或可通过专门的摆渡工具实现旅客换乘衔接。

北京市目前主要有四类客运枢纽，具体如下：

（1）包含铁路与公交、地铁、出租四种运输方式的客运枢纽：如北京南站、北京西客站等。

（2）包含公路客运与公交、地铁三种运输方式的客运枢纽：如六里桥客运枢纽。

（3）包含民航与机场巴士、公交、地铁、出租五种运输方式的客运枢纽：如首都机场等。

（4）包含公交与地铁两种运输方式的客运枢纽：如东直门客运枢纽。

省际客运运营线路条数：指报告期末，省际客运企业实际经营的客运班线条数。计量单位：条。

省际客运运营线路长度：指报告期末，省际客运企业实际经营的客运班线长度之和。计量单位：公里。

客运班线平均日发班次：指报告期内，本辖区内所有班车平均每日实际开行的班次数。计量单位：班次/日。县内班车往返一趟计算两个班次。两天一班计1/2个班次，三天一班计1/3个班次。

客运站平均日旅客发送量：指报告期内，本辖区内取得经营许可的客运站平均每日发送的旅客人数。计量单位：人次。

客运量：指报告期内实际运送的旅客人数。计量单位：万人次。

旅客周转量：指报告期内，实际运送的每位乘客与其相应运送距离的乘积之和。计量单位：万人公里。

计算公式：旅客周转量 = ∑（实际运送的每位旅客 × 该旅客出发站与到达站间的距离）。

统计分组：公路旅客周转量按省际客运、旅游客运、郊区客运分别统计。

道路运输从业人员：指报告期末，在道路运输业中从事生产、经营和管理的人员数。计量单位：人。

计算方法：道路运输从业人员数按辖区内道路运输行业所有经营业户的实际从业人员数来统计。其中从事道路危险货物运输的驾驶人员、押运人员和装卸管理人员指经所在地设区的市级人民政府交通主管部门考试合格并取得相应从业资格证的人员。

统计范围：道路运输从业人员数不包括城市客运从业人员数量。

统计分组：根据经营范围按省际客运、旅游客运、郊区客运、货物运输、汽车租赁、机动车维修及汽车综合性能检测站从业人员分别统计。

公路运输车辆数：指报告期末，从事公路旅客运输或货物运输的各类运输车辆的实有数量。计量单位：辆。

统计分组：一般按以下方式分组：
（1）按运输车辆的车体结构分。
（2）按运输车辆的经营范围和用途分。
（3）按运输车辆使用的能源种类分。
（4）按运输车辆的技术特征分。
（5）按车辆的营运方式分。

其中，载客汽车一般按以下方式分组：
（1）按标记客位分为：大型客车、中型客车、小型客车。
（2）按车长分为：特大型客车、大型客车、中型客车、小型客车。
（3）按等级分为：高级客车、中级客车、普通客车。

（4）按燃料类型分为：汽油车、柴油车、液化石油气车、天然气车、双燃料车、纯电动车、混合动力车、其他燃料车。
（5）按经营范围分为：班车客车、旅游客车、包车客车、其他客车。

其中，载货汽车一般按以下方式分组：
（1）按车型结构分为：栏板车、厢式车、集装箱车和罐车。
（2）按经营范围分为：普通载货汽车和专用载货汽车。
（3）按标记吨位分为：大型（含重型）车、中型车和小型车。
（4）按燃料类型分为：汽油车、柴油车、液化石油气车、天然气车、双燃料车、纯电动车、混合动力车、其他燃料车。

车辆客位数：指报告期末，载客车辆的标记或核定客位，反映载客车辆的运载能力。计量单位：客位。

车辆吨位数：指报告期末，载货车辆的标记或核定吨位，反映载货车辆的运载能力。计量单位：吨位。

经营业户数：持有道路运输管理机构核发的道路运输经营许可证，或者在交通运输行业管理机构备案，或者纳入交通运输行业管理，从事道路运输业务或相关业务经营活动的业户数。计量单位：户。

统计分组：根据经营范围按省际客运、旅游客运、郊区客运、货物运输、汽车租赁、机动车维修及汽车综合性能检测站七类分别统计。

机动车维修完成主要工作量：指报告期内各类机动车维修业户完成的主要维修工作量。计量单位：辆（台）次。

统计分组：机动车维修完成主要工作量按整车修理、总成修理、二级维护、专项修理和维修救援五类分别统计。

汽车综合性能检测站数量：按照规定的程序和方法，通过一系列技术操作行为，对在用汽车综合性能（指在用汽车动力性、安全性、燃料经济性、使用可靠性、排气污染物和噪声以及整车装备完整性与状态、防雨密封性等多种技术性能的组合）进行检测（验）评价工作并提供检测数据、报告的社会化服务机构数量。计量单位：个。

完成检测量：指报告期内各类取得经营许可的汽车综合性能检测站完成的各类检测辆次数。计量单位：辆次。

汽车租赁率：指已出租车辆与租赁车辆的比率。计量单位：%。

计算公式：汽车租赁率 = 已出租车辆/租赁车辆数 × 100%。

Explanatory Notes on Main Statistical Indicators

Number of rail transit stations refers to the number of places along the operating rail transit routes for passengers to wait and get in and off the train at the end of the report period. Unit: unit.

Number of rail transit transfer stations refers to the number of stations along the rail transit routes at the end of the report period where passengers can transfer from one rail transit route to another through the same platform or a dedicated channel. Unit: unit.

Calculation method: The transfer stations of different rail transit routes is counted as one.

Number of rail transit operating routes refers to the total number of fixed routes set for rail transit operating trains at the end of the report period. Unit: route.

Calculation method: The route which is designed as the same route but built by stages should be calculated as one route.

Statistical grouping: Rail transit operating routes are generally include metro, light rail, monorail, tram and magnetically suspension train, etc.

Total length of rail transit operating routes refers to the sum of lengths of all rail transit routes at the end of the report period, including ground route, underground route and elevated route, excluding non-operational routes such as turn line, test line and contact line. Unit: km.

Statistical grouping: The same as number of rail transit operating routes.

Number of rail transit operating vehicles refers to the total number of vehicles used for rail transit operations in the city at the end of the report period. Unit: vehicle.

Calculation method: Based on the number of vehicles which has already put into operation in the fixed assets account of the enterprise (unit); the newly purchased, newly manufactured and transferred-in operating vehicles will be counted from the date it is put into use; operational vehicles that transferred out, scrapped or transferred for other purposes should not be included from the date of approval by the competent authorities at the higher levels. In the statistics of metro, light rail, monorail and magnetically suspension train, one natural section is one vehicle, which is out of accordance with marshalling train. The rail transit system shall be classified and definited according to *Standard for Classification of Urban Public Transportation (CJJ/ T 114—2007)*.

Number of rail transit standard operating vehicles refers to the number of operating vehicles converted from rail transit operating vehicles of different types by unified standard equivalent at the end of the report period. Unit: standard vehicle.

Calculation formula: the number of rail transit standard operating vehicles (standard station) = Σ (number of vehicles of each type × corresponding conversion coefficient).

Number of rail transit marshalling refers to the total number of marshalling trains of each rail transit operating route within the jurisdiction at the end of the report period. Unit: unit.

Rail transit rated passenger capacity refers to the total number of rated passenger capacity of all rail transit operating vehicles at the end of the report period. Unit of: person.

Maximum load rate of rail transit during the peak hours, which is also called the maximum load rate of section during peak hours, refers to the ratio between the one-way maximum section passenger flow of the rail transit line during the peak period and the transport capacity of this section. Unit: %.

Rail transit passenger traffic refers to the total number of passengers transported by rail transit during the report period, including paying passengers and non-paying passengers. Unit: 10 000 person-times.

Rail transit passenger turnover refers to the sum of the transported passengers multiplied by the transport distance during the report period. Unit: 10 000 person-km.

Average daily passenger traffic of rail transit refers to the average daily number of passenger transported by rail transit during the report period. Unit: 10 000 person-times.

Number of public trolley buses refers to the number of all public trolley buses used for public passenger transportation operation service by cities (counties) at the end of the report period. Unit: vehicle.

Calculation method: The newly purchased, newly manufactured and transferred-in operating vehicles will be counted from the date it is put into use; operational vehicles that transferred out, scrapped or transferred for other purposes should not be included from the date of approval by the competent authorities at the higher levels. Statistics can be done according to length of vehicle, fuel types, emission standards and whether the vehicle is equipped with air condition.

Statistical grouping: generally grouped as follows:

(1) By length, for example, $\leq$ 5 meters, $>$ 5 meters and $\leq$ 7 meters, $>$ 7 meters and $\leq$ 10 meters, $>$ 10 meters and $\leq$ 13 meters, $>$ 13 meters and $\leq$ 16 meters, $>$ 16 meters and $\leq$ 18 meters, $>$ 18 meters, double deck bus.

(2) By fuel type, for example, gasoline vehicles, ethanol gasoline vehicles, diesel vehicles, liquefied petroleum gas vehicles, natural gas vehicles, dual-fuel vehicles, trolleybuses, battery electric vehicle, hybrid vehicles and other fuel vehicles.

(3) By emission standard, for example, National grade II and below, National grade III, National grade IV, National grade V and above, zero emissions.

(4) By driving area, for example, urban bus and suburban bus.

Number of trolley buses standard operating vehicles refers to the number of operating vehicles converted from trolley buses operating vehicles of different types by unified standard equivalent at the end of the report period. Unit of measurement: standard vehicle.

Calculation formula: Number of standard operating vehicles (standard vehicle) = Σ (number of vehicles of each type × corresponding conversion coefficient).

Trolley bus rated passenger capacity refers to the total number of rated passenger capacity of all trolley bus operating vehicles at the end of the report period, also called verified passenger capacity. Unit: person.

Calculation formula: Trolley bus rated passenger capacity = fixed passenger seat number + effective standing area (square meters) × number of people allowed to stand per square meter.

Operating length of public trolley bus refers to the total distance traveled by trolley buses for operation during the report period. Unit of measurement: km.

Statistical scope: The operating length of public trolley bus includes carrying kilometres and deadhead kilometres, excluding the mileage for maintenance, repair or test. Carrying kilometres refers to the distance traveled by operating vehicles to carry passengers, including the distance traveled by operating vehicles to carry passengers on the routes and the distance traveled by chartered vehicles. Deadhead kilometres refers to the distance traveled by an empty vehicle which is not allowed to carry passengers according to regulation, including the distance traveled between the vehicle yard and the route, halfway broken-down, the distance traveled to the start point, the terminal point or the vehicle yard for other reasons, also including the distance traveled on the return journey.

Number of operating taxi refers the number of operating vehicles that have obtained a special license for taxi at the end of the report period, including vehicles that are in good condition, under repair, after long-term use and those intended to be scrapped but have not yet been approved by the authorities of higher level. Unit: vehicle.

Statistical range: Taxis generally meeting the fonowing requirements. The technical performance and facilities of the vehicles are intact, and the vehicles are kept clean and tidy; The taxi shall be equipped with a taximeter approved by the passenger transport management authority and certified as qualified by the technical supervision department; Small taxicar shall be equipped with security facilities for preventing looting which have been certified as qualified by the public security organs; The taxi shall be fixed with uniform overhead lights and clear signs showing empty vehicles for rent. The term "individual taxi" refers to a taxi operating as an individual, which has a special taxi license plate and a business license.

Statistical grouping: Generally grouped as follows:

(1) By fuel type, for example, gasoline vehicles, ethanol gasoline vehicles, diesel vehicles, liquefied petroleum gas vehicles, natural gas vehicles, dual fuel vehicles, battery electric vehicles and other fuel vehicles.

(2) By operation modes, for example, individual taxi and non-individual taxi.

Operating length of taxi refers to the total distance travelled by taxies for passenger transportation during the report period, including passenger kilometres and deadhead kilometres. Unit: 10 000 km.

Passenger kilometres of taxi refers to the mileage that taxies for passenger transportation provide passenger services as the passenger wishes and charge fees. Unit: 10 000 km.

Calculation formula: Passenger kilometres of taxi =

number of the speedometer when passengers get off – number of the speedometer when passengers get in.

Passenger traffic of public trolley buses refers to the total number of passengers transported by public trolley buses during the report period, including paying passengers and non-paying passengers. Unit of measurement: 10 000 person-times.

Passenger traffic of taxi refers to the total number of passengers transported by taxies during the report period. Unit of measurement: 10 000 person-times.

Calculation formula: Passenger Traffic = Total number of passenger carrying vehicle capacity × Passenger carrying capacity coefficient.

Each enterprise may determine the passenger carrying coefficient according to the actual passenger flow survey data. If there is no relevant survey data, it can be calculated as 2 passengers per vehicle.

Number of public trolley buses operating routes refers to the total number of fixed routes set for trolley buses at the end of the report period. Unit: line.

Statistical range: The number of public trolley buses operating routes includes the number of main lines, branch lines, special lines and fixed lines for peak hours, excluding the number of temporary lines and joint lines.

Statistical grouping: Generally grouped as follows:

(1) By region: Number of urban trolley bus routes, number of suburban trolley bus routes.

(2) By ticket system: Number of operating practising sectional fare and number of operation practising full fare.

Total length of public trolley buses operating routes refers to the sum of lengths of all public trolley buses routes at the end of the report period. Unit: km.

Statistical range: The total length of public trolley buses operating routes does not include Non-operating routes such as return route, test route or contact routes.

Number of public trolley buses employees refers to the actual number of persons who work for trolley buses proprietor and receive remuneration at the end of the report period. Unit: person.

Statistical grouping: Generally according to the position of the employees, such as the number of drivers, conductors, stewards and so on.

Number of taxi employees refers to the actual number of persons who work for taxi proprietor and receive remuneration at the end of the report period. Unit: person.

Statistical grouping: Generally according to the position of the employees, such as number of drivers, financial personnel and soon.

Number of passenger stations refers to the number of passenger stations that have been approved by the transportation management authority and obtained business license at the end of the report period. Unit: unit.

The number of passenger stations is calculated by the station grade according to *Classification and Facilities Requirements of Road Passenger Station (JT/T 200—2004)* issued by the Ministry of Transport.

Statistical grouping: Divided into first grade station, second grade station, third grade station, fourth grade station, fifth grade station, simple station and request stop by the passenger station grades.

Passenger transportation hub refers to a transport system that includes multiple modes of passenger transport, which can realize seamless transfer, and has one or more basic functions such as transport organization and management, passenger transfer, multimodal transport, communication information and support services for production and life. Unit: unit.

Passenger transportation hub is a large passenger flow distribution point where multiple passenger transport routes converge. The physical buildings of terminal facilities with different modes of transport in the hub station should be set up or connected with special channels within the same space or connected by special ferry tools.

Currently, Beijing has four major passenger transportation hubs, as follows:

(1) Passenger transportation hubs with four transport methods including railway, bus, subway and taxi, such as Beijing South Railway Station and Beijing West Railway Station.

(2) Passenger transportation hubs with three transport methods including highway, bus and subway, such as Liuliqiao Passenger Transportation Hub.

(3) Passenger transport hubs with five transport methods including civil aviation, airport bus, bus, subway and taxi, such as Capital Airport.

(4) Passenger transportation hubs with two transport methods including bus and subway, such as Dongzhimen Passenger Transportation Hub.

Number of Interprovincial passenger transportation routes refers to the number of passenger transportation routes actually operated by interprovincial passenger transportation enterprises at the end of the reporting period. Unit: route.

Length of interprovincial passenger transportation routes refers to the total length of passenger transportation routes actually operated by interprovincial passenger transport enterprises at the end of the reporting period. Unit: km.

Average daily dispatched runs of passenger transportation routes refers to the average number of daily actual departures of all regular buses within the jurisdiction during the report period. Unit: run/day. One round trip for intra-county bus is counted as two runs. Two-day run is counted as 1/2 and Three-day run is counted as 1/3.

Number of average daily dispatched passenger of passenger stations refers to the average daily number of passenger dispatched from passenger stations with business licenses within the juris diction during the report period. Unit: person-time.

Passenger traffic refers to the actual number of passengers transported during the report period. Unit: 10 000 person-time.

Passenger turnover refers to the sum of the passengers carried actually by all operating vehicles multiplied by the corresponding transport distance during the report period. Unit: 10 000 person-km.

The formula: Passenger Turnover (person-km) = $\sum$ (actually transported passenger × the distance traveled by the passenger).

Statistical grouping: Divided into interprovincial passenger transportation, tourist passenger transportation and suburban passenger transportation.

Number of road transportation employees refers to the number of persons engaged in production, operation and management of the road transport at the end of the report period. Unit: person.

Calculation method: The number of road transportation employees is calculated according to the number of actual employees of all the road transport businesses within the jurisdiction. Among them, the drivers engaged in dangerous goods transportation, escorts and handling personnel refer to the persons who pass the examination and obtain the corresponding qualification certificate by the competent administrative department for transportation under the people's government of district-constituted municipalities.

Statistical scope: The number of road transportation employees does not include the number of urban passenger transportation employees.

Statistics grouping: Divided into employees of interprovincial passenger transportation, tourist passenger transportation, suburban passenger transportation,freight transportation, vehicle rental, motor vehicle maintenance and synthetic vehicle performance test station.

Number of highway transportation vehicles refers to the actual number of various types of transport vehicles used for highway passengers transportation or freight transportation at the end of the report period. Unit: vehicle.

Statistical grouping: Generally grouped as follows:

(1) By the structure of transport vehicles.

(2) By the business scope and use of transport vehicles.

(3) By fuel type of transport vehicles.

(4) By technical characteristics of transport vehicles.

(5) By the operation manner of transport vehicles.

Among them, passenger vehicles are generally grouped as follows:

(1) By rated seat: Large passenger vehicles, medium passenger vehicles and mini passenger vehicles.

(2) By vehicle length: Extra-large passenger vehicles, large passenger vehicles, medium passenger vehicles and mini passenger vehicles.

(3) By class: High-class passenger vehicles, middle-class passenger vehicles and ordinary-class passenger vehicles.

(4) By fuel types: Gasoline vehicles, diesel vehicles, liquefied petroleum vehicles, natural gas vehicles, dual-fuel vehicles, battery electric vehicles, hybrid vehicles and other fuel vehicles.

(5) By business scope: regular vehicles, tourist vehicles, chartered vehicles and other vehicles.

Among them, the freight vehicles are generally grouped as follows:

(1) By the structure: Tailgate truck, van, container truck and tank truck.

(2) By business scope: Common truck and special truck.

(3) By tonnage: large truck (including heavy truck), medium truck and light truck.

(4) By fuel types: gasoline vehicles, diesel vehicles, liquefied petroleum vehicles, natural gas vehicles, dual-fuel vehicles, battery electric vehicles, hybrid vehicles and other fuel vehicles.

Vehicle passenger seat refers to the marked or approved seats of passenger vehicles at the end of the report period, reflecting the carrying capacity of passenger vehicles. Unit: seat.

Vehicle tonnage refers to the marked or approved tonnage of the freight vehicles at the end of the report period, reflecting the carrying capacity of the vehicle. Unit: tonnage.

Number of Business Operators refers to those who hold road transport operation licenses issued by road transport management agencies, or filed with transport industry management agencies, or incorporated into transport industry management and engage in road transport business or related business operations. Unit: unit.

Statistics grouping: Divided into seven categories, such as interprovincial passenger transportation, tourist passenger transportation, suburban passenger transportation, freight transportation, vehicle rental, motor vehicle maintenance and synthetic vehicle performance test station.

Major workload of motor vehicle maintenance refers to the main workload completed by various motor vehicle maintenance operators during the report period. Unit: vehicles (stations)-time.

Statistical grouping: Divided into five categories, such as vehicle repair, assembly repair, secondary maintenance, special repair and maintenance rescue.

Number of synthetic vehicle performance test station refers to the social service organizations which test and evaluate comprehensive performance of the vehicle in use (refers to the combination of power performance, safety, fuel economy, operational reliability, exhaust pollutants and noise, equipment integrity and state, rain proof tightness and other technical performances) and provide test data and reports according to regulated procedure and method by a series of technical operation behaviors. Unit:unit.

Detection amount refers to the sum of vehicle detection that synthetic vehicle performance test station actually completed during the report period. Unit:vehicle-time.

Car rental rate refers to the ratio of rented vehicles to vehicles for hire. Unit:%.

Calculating formula: Car rental rate = Number of rented vehicles / Number of vehicles for hire × 100%.

五、货物运输
FREIGHT TRANSPORTATION

简 要 说 明
Brief Introduction

本篇资料反映北京市公路货运发展的基本情况，主要包括：公路货物运输量、集装箱运输量及运输装备。

Statistics in this chapter reflects the development situation of highway freight transportation of Beijing, mainly including highway freight traffic, container traffic and transportation equipments.

5-1 货 物 运 输
Freight Transportation

指标 Indicator		计量单位 Unit		数量 Number
基础设施	Infrastructure	–	–	–
货运站数量	Freight station	个	unit	9
一级站	First-grade Station	个	unit	1
二级站	Second-grade Station	个	unit	–
三级站	Third-grade Station	个	unit	8
四级站	Fourth-grade Station	个	unit	–
货运枢纽总计	Freight Transportation Hub	个	unit	–
运输服务	Transportation Service	–	–	–
货运量	Freight Traffic	万吨	10,000 tons	20 278
货物周转量	Turnover of Freight Traffic	万吨公里	10,000 tons-kms	1 674 068
道路货物运输经营业户数	Number of Road Freight Transportation Operators	户	unit	**43 436**
其中：普通货运	of which: General Freight Transportation	户	unit	42 116
货物专用运输	Special Freight Transportation	户	unit	3 283
内：集装箱运输	including: Container Transportation	户	unit	727
大型物件运输	Large Article Transportation	户	unit	273
道路货物运输相关业务经营业户数	Number of Related Business Operators	户	unit	**784**
其中：货运站（场）	of which: Freight Station	户	unit	9
货运代办	Freight Forwarder	户	unit	775
从业人员数	Number of Employees	人	person	**406 137**
其中：道路货物运输驾驶员	of which: Road Freight Transportation Drivers	人	person	359 486

5-2 公路货物营运车辆拥有量（按标记吨位分）
Possession of Commercial Highway Freight Vehicles (By Capacity Tonnage)

指标 Indicator	计算单位 Unit	总计 Total	按标记吨位分 (By Capacity Tonnage)			
			大型 Large	重型 Heavy	中型 Medium	小型 Light
总计 Total	辆 vehicle	168 626	–	–	–	–
	吨位 tonnage	964 320	–	–	–	–
载货汽车 Freight Vehicle	辆 vehicle	168 626	68 082	31 946	4 022	96 408
	吨位 tonnage	964 320	814 788	560 245	14 634	134 898
1. 货车 1.Truck	辆 vehicle	161 925	61 515	25 391	4 011	96 399
	吨位 tonnage	763 185	613 701	359 209	14 598	134 886
按车型结构分 By Vehicle Structure	–	–	–	–	–	–
普通货车 Common Truck	辆 vehicle	1 199	535	399	48	616
	吨位 tonnage	9 997	8 915	7 911	188	894
平板货车 Flatbed Truck	辆 vehicle	56 424	17 034	1 557	1 781	37 609
	吨位 tonnage	190 859	126 977	24 354	6 639	57 243
仓栅式货车 Box Truck	辆 vehicle	7 924	6 026	892	20	1 878
	吨位 tonnage	58 097	55 063	15 163	75	2 959
厢式货车 Van	辆 vehicle	66 048	21 180	6 349	1 856	43 012
	吨位 tonnage	258 637	189 620	82 176	6 712	62 305
其中：冷藏保温车 of which: Refrigerated Truck	辆 vehicle	7 739	1 896	438	810	5 033
	吨位 tonnage	25 430	16 228	5 875	2 988	6 214
封闭货车 Closed Truck	辆 vehicle	11 181	21	16	30	11 130
	吨位 tonnage	9 014	750	725	82	8 182
罐式货车 Tank Truck	辆 vehicle	6 398	6 220	5 916	129	49
	吨位 tonnage	98 870	98 357	96 364	421	92
特殊结构货车 Special Construction Truck	辆 vehicle	1 365	1 172	1 144	42	151
	吨位 tonnage	14 494	14 155	13 984	128	211
自卸货车 Dump Truck	辆 vehicle	11 386	9 327	9 118	105	1 954
	吨位 tonnage	123 217	119 864	118 532	353	3 000
按经营范围分 By Business Scope	–	–	–	–	–	–
普通载货汽车 Common Truck	辆 vehicle	146 127	53 198	19 082	2 817	90 112
	吨位 tonnage	648 711	511 395	272 316	10 273	127 043
专用载货汽车 Special Truck	辆 vehicle	15 798	8 317	6 309	1 194	6 287
	吨位 tonnage	114 474	102 306	86 893	4 325	7 843
其中：商品汽车运输车 of which: Merchandise Car Transporter	辆 vehicle	–	–	–	–	–
	吨位 tonnage	–	–	–	–	–
大型物件运输车 Large Object Transporter	辆 vehicle	11	8	8	3	–

5-2 （续表一）

指标 Indicator		计算单位 Unit		总计 Total	按标记吨位分 (By Capacity Tonnage)			
					大型 Large	重型 Heavy	中型 Medium	小型 Light
		吨位	tonnage	294	284	284	10	–
按燃料类型分	By Fuel Type	–	–	–	–	–	–	–
汽油车	Gasoline Vehicle	辆	vehicle	30 898	–	–	–	–
柴油车	Diesel Vehicle	辆	vehicle	125 703	–	–	–	–
液化石油汽车	Liquefied Petroleum Vehicle	辆	vehicle	2	–	–	–	–
天然气车	Natural Gas Vehicle	辆	vehicle	711	–	–	–	–
纯电动车	Battery Electric Vehicle	辆	vehicle	4 540	–	–	–	–
其他燃料车	Others	辆	vehicle	71	–	–	–	–
2.牵引车	2.Tractor	辆	vehicle	114	–	–	–	–
（1）按燃料类型分	By Fuel Type	–	–	–	–	–	–	–
汽油车	Gasoline Vehicle	辆	vehicle		–	–	–	–
柴油车	Diesel Vehicle	辆	vehicle	113	–	–	–	–
天然气车	Natural Gas Vehicle	辆	vehicle	1	–	–	–	–
3.挂车	3.Trailer	辆	vehicle	6 587	6 567	6 555	11	9
		吨位	tonnage	201 135	201 087	201 036	36	12
（1）按车型结构分	（1）By Vehicle Structure	–	–	–	–	–	–	–
普通挂车	Common Trailer	辆	vehicle	2 050	2 041	2 029	8	1
		吨位	tonnage	55 969	55 942	55 891	26	1
平板挂车	Flatbed Trailer	辆	vehicle	998	990	990	–	8
		吨位	tonnage	29 233	29 222	29 222	–	11
集装箱挂车	Container Trailer	辆	vehicle	3 539	3 536	3 536	3	–
		吨位	tonnage	115 933	115 923	115 923	10	–
		TEU	TEU	7 729.00	7 728.00	7 728.00	1.00	0.00
（2）按经营范围分	（2）By Business Scope	–	–	–	–	–	–	–
普通载货汽车	Common Freight Vehicle	辆	vehicle	3 123	3 114	3 113	8	1
		吨位	tonnage	87 452	87 425	87 419	26	1
专用载货汽车	Special Freight Vehicle	辆	vehicle	3 464	3 453	3 442	3	8
		吨位	tonnage	113 683	113 662	113 617	10	11
其中：商品汽车运输	of which: Merchandise Car Transporter	辆	vehicle	–	–	–	–	–
		吨位	tonnage	–	–	–	–	–
大型物件运输	Large Object Transporter	辆	vehicle	419	419	419	–	–
		吨位	tonnage	11 908	11 908	11 908	–	–

5-3 公路货物营运
Possession of Commercial Highway

指标 Indicator		单位计量 Unit		总计 Total
货车	Truck	辆	vehicle	161 925
		吨位	tonnage	1 594 457
按车型结构分	By Vehicle Structure	—	—	—
普通货车	Common Truck	辆	vehicle	1 199
		吨位	tonnage	14 464
平板货车	Flatbed Truck	辆	vehicle	56 424
		吨位	tonnage	405 394
仓栅式货车	Box Truck	辆	vehicle	7 924
		吨位	tonnage	113 039
厢式货车	Van	辆	vehicle	66 048
		吨位	tonnage	558 235
其中：冷藏保温车	Of which: Refrigerated Truck	辆	vehicle	7 739
		吨位	tonnage	60 025
封闭货车	Closed Truck	辆	vehicle	11 181
		吨位	tonnage	29 205
罐式货车	Tank Truck	辆	vehicle	6 398
		吨位	tonnage	193 581
特殊结构货车	Special Construction Truck	辆	vehicle	1 365
		吨位	tonnage	35 105
自卸货车	Dump Truck	辆	vehicle	11 386
		吨位	tonnage	245 434
按经营范围分	By Business Scope	—	—	—
普通载货汽车	Common Freight Vehicle	辆	vehicle	146 127
		吨位	tonnage	1 408 582
专用载货汽车	Special Freight Vehicle	辆	vehicle	15 798
		吨位	tonnage	185 875
其中：商品汽车运输车	of which: Merchandise Car Transporter	辆	vehicle	—
		吨位	tonnage	
大型物件运输车	Large Object Transporter	辆	vehicle	11
		吨位	tonnage	319

车辆拥有量（按总质量分）
Freight Vehicles (By Total Mass)

按总质量分 By Total Mass					安装卫星定位车载终端 Equipped with Satellite Positioning Vehicle Terminals	重型车辆 Heavy Vehicle
重型 Heavy	特重型 Extra-heavy	中型 Medium	轻型 Light	微型 Mini		
56 286	23 932	9 304	92 813	3 522	56 286	56 286
1 144 805	649 147	83 167	360 566	5 919	1 144 805	1 144 805
-	-	-	-	-	-	-
530	237	100	566	3	530	530
11 678	6 683	832	1 952	2	11 678	11 678
14 658	1 211	4 125	36 631	1 010	14 658	14 658
233 623	32 121	35 925	134 181	1 665	233 623	233 623
5 931	836	255	1 736	2	5 931	5 931
103 120	23 621	2 365	7 551	3	103 120	103 120
18 532	5 604	4 435	42 895	186	18 532	18 532
334 412	135 827	40 717	182 780	326	334 412	334 412
1 602	303	1 100	4 946	91	1 602	1 602
28 924	8 404	9 592	21 346	163	28 924	28 924
7	6	8	8 847	2 319	7	7
168	155	53	25 063	3 921	168	168
6 208	5 774	156	34	-	6 208	6 208
192 073	183 520	1 356	152	-	192 073	192 073
1 179	1 135	39	147	-	1 179	1 179
34 222	33 667	257	626	-	34 222	34 222
9 241	9 129	186	1 957	2	9 241	9 241
235 509	233 553	1 662	8 261	2	235 509	235 509
-	-	-	-	-	-	-
49 842	17 780	5 798	87 087	3 400	49 842	49 842
1 006 870	516 450	60 241	335 766	5 705	1 006 870	1 006 870
6 444	6 152	3 506	5 726	122	6 444	6 444
137 935	132 697	22 926	24 800	214	137 935	137 935
-	-	-	-	-	-	-
-	-	-	-	-	-	-
8	4	3	-	-	8	8
295	215	24	-	-	295	295

主要统计指标解释
Explanatory Notes on Main Statistical Indicators

货运站数量：指报告期末，经交通运输管理机构核定并取得经营许可的货运站数量。计量单位：个。

货运站数量按站级统计，站级划分按部颁标准《汽车货运站（场）级别划分和建设要求》（JT/T 402—1999）执行。

统计分组：按货运站的等级分为：一级站、二级站、三级站和四级站。

货运量：指报告期内，运输车辆实际运送的货物重量。计量单位：万吨。

货物周转量：指报告期内，运输车辆实际运送的每批货物重量与其相应运送距离的乘积之和。计量单位：万吨公里。

计算公式：货物周转量（吨公里）= ∑（运送的每批货物重量 × 该批货物的运送距离）。

货物运输经营业户数：指报告期末，持有道路运输管理机构核发的道路运输经营许可证，所有从事道路货物运输经营活动的企业和个体运输户的数量。计量单位：户。

道路货物运输相关业务经营业户数：持有道路货物运输管理机构核发的道路运输经营许可证，或者在交通运输行业管理机构备案，或者纳入交通运输行业管理，从事道路货物运输相关业务经营活动的业户数。计量单位：户。

货运代办：指受货物收货人、发货人的委托，以委托人或自己的名义，为委托人办理货物运输及相关业务，并收取劳务报酬的行为。通常货运代办方为中间人而非承运人。计量单位：户。

Number of freight stations refers to the number of freight stations that have been approved by the transportation management authority and obtained business license at the end of the reporting period. Unit:unit.

The number of freight stations is calculated by the station grade, and the station grade shall be divided according to *Classification and Construction Requirements of Freight Terminal (JT/T 402—1999)* issued by the Ministry of Transport.

Statistical grouping: Divided into first grade station, second grade station, third grade station and fourth grade station according to the freight station grades.

Freight traffic refers to the actual weight of the cargo carried by the transportation vehicles during the reporting period. Unit of measurement: 10 000 tons.

Freight turnover refers to the sum of the actual weight of each shipment carried by transportation vehicles multiplied by the corresponding transport distance during the reporting period. Unit of measurement: 10 000 ton-km.

Formula: Freight Turnover (ton-km) = $\sum$ (weight of each shipment × the transport distance of the shipment).

Number of road freight transportation operators refers to the number of all enterprises and individual transport operators engaged in the road freight transportation business activities which hold the road transport business license issued by the road transport management authority, at the end of the report period. Unit: unit.

Number of business operators related to road freight transportation refers to the number of those who hold road freight transport business licenses issued by road freight transport management agencies, or filed with transport industry management agencies, or incorporated into transport industry management and engage in road freight transport related business operations. Unit: household.

Freight forwarder refers to the act of handling cargo transportation and related business for clients and collect remuneration for services in the name of the client or himself, entrusted by the consignee or consignor of the goods. Freight forwarders are usually intermediaries rather than carriers. Unit: household.

六、路网运行
ROAD NETWORK

简 要 说 明
Brief Introduction

一、本篇资料反映北京市路网运行的基本情况。主要包括公路交通情况观测站点、公路年平均日交通量等统计资料。

I.Statistics in this chapter reflects the basic situation of road network in Beijing, mainly including highway traffic observation station, highway traffic annual average daily traffic volume and so on.

二、调查站点数量指报告期末，辖区内所有交通量调查站点的数量。交通量指在单位时间内，通过公路某一断面的实际车辆数。

II. Number of survey stations refers to the number of all traffic survey stations within the jurisdiction at the end of the report period. Traffic volume refers to the actual number of vehicles passing through a cross-section of the highway in unit time.

6-1 公路交通调查管理情况
Highway Traffic Survey Management

指标 Indicator		计量单位 Unit		数 量 Number
调查统计管理机构数	Number of Administrative Organizations of Survey Statistics	个	unit	24
省级	Provincial-level	个	unit	8
地市级	Prefecture-level	个	unit	16
县乡级	County-level	个	unit	-
观测点数量	Number of Observation Stations	个	unit	659
按所在公路等级分	By the Grade of the Highway	-	-	-
国道	National Highway	个	unit	124
省道	Provincial Highway	个	unit	152
县道	County Highway	个	unit	383
按站点类型等级分	By Type of Observation Stations	-	-	-
连续式	Continuous Type	个	unit	501
间歇式	Intermittent Type	个	unit	156
比重调查	Proportion Survey	个	unit	2
车速调查路段	Speed Survey Section	个	unit	173
国道	National Highway	个	unit	18
省道	Provincial Highway	个	unit	41
县道	County Highway	个	unit	114
观测人员数量	Number of Observers	人	person	310
交调设备数量	Quantity of Traffic Survey Equipment	台/套	piece/set	502

6-2 国家高速
National Expressway

路线编号 Route Number	路线名称 Route Name		观测里程（公里）Observation Mileage (km)	行驶量（万车公里/日）Vehicle Travel (10 000 vehicle-km/day)	适应交通量（辆/日）Adaptable Daily Traffic (vehicle/day)	地点车速（公里/时）Spot Speed (km/h)
	合　计	Total	395.9	2 553.0	0.9	69.0
G1	北京－哈尔滨高速公路	Beijing–Harbin Expressway	29.1	153.0	0.5	68.3
G2	北京－上海高速公路	Beijing–Shanghai Expressway	4.2	44.0	1.9	－
G3	北京－台北高速公路	Beijing–Taibei Expressway	12.2	58.0	0.9	96.6
G4	北京－港澳高速公路	Beijing – Hong Kong – Macao Expressway	30.7	258.0	1.1	75.5
G5	北京－昆明高速公路	Beijing–Kunming Expressway	26.0	78.0	0.5	81.0
G6	北京－拉萨高速公路	Beijing–Lhasa Expressway	61.0	510.0	1.0	59.6
G7	北京－乌鲁木齐高速公路	Beijing–Urumqi Expressway	7.0	8.0	0.2	69.5
G45	大庆－广州高速公路	Daqing – Guangzhou Expressway	130.7	1 052.0	1.0	67.5
G4501	北京六环高速	6th Ring Road Expressway of Beijing	95.0	392.0	0.9	－

公路交通量
Traffic

		汽车平均日交通量（辆/日） Average Daily Vehicle Traffic (vehicle/day)						
当量合计 Total of Equivalent	自然合计 Total of Natural Number	小型货车 Mini Truck	中型货车 Medium Truck	大型货车 Large Truck	特大货车 Extra-large Truck	集装箱车 Container Car	中小客车 Mini-medium Bus	大客车 Large Bus
64 530	**49 501**	**3 737**	**2 921**	**1 692**	**2 036**	**1 039**	**36 157**	**1 919**
52 771	38 666	2 365	2 115	1 509	2 229	941	28 467	1 040
103 407	82 899	1 115	1 125	4 988	1 081	1 796	70 117	2 677
47 605	39 073	2 539	2 326	701	1 738	167	31 097	505
84 209	69 905	6 712	3 651	1 041	2 263	773	52 888	2 577
29 911	21 129	1 849	916	576	2 280	50	15 093	365
83 737	64 961	4 261	3 585	2 105	3 021	826	48 698	2 465
11 630	4 519	205	489	256	2 006	108	1 430	25
80 544	59 844	4 505	4 202	2 278	2 313	1 831	41 493	3 222
41 267	33 029	2 854	1 627	1 283	908	620	25 188	549

6-3 普通国
Ordinary National

路线编号 Route Number	路线名称 Route Name		观测里程（公里） Observation Mileage (km)	机动车平均日交通量（辆/日） Average Daily Motor Vehicle Traffic (vehicle/day)		行驶量（万车公里/日） Vehicle Travel (10 000 vehicle-km/day)	适应交通量（辆/日） Adaptable Daily Traffic (vehicle/day)	交通拥挤度 Traffic Congestion Degrees
				当量合计 Total of Equivalent	自然合计 Total of Natural Number			
	合 计	Total	760.7	11 571	8 768	875.0	0.6	0.7
G101	北京－沈阳公路	Beijing–Shenyang Highway	78.7	21 784	14 120	171.0	0.7	0.7
G102	北京－抚远公路	Beijing–Fuyuan Highway	6.8	53 025	47 326	36.0	1.2	1.2
G103	北京－滨海新区	Beijing–Binhaixinqu Highway	23.2	68 048	54 489	158.0	1.5	2.4
G104	北京－平潭公路	Beijing–Pingtan Highway	14.5	24 626	20 285	36.0	1.2	1.3
G106	北京－广州公路	Beijing–Guangzhou Highway	8.9	63 063	47 978	56.0	1.1	1.2
G107	北京－深圳公路	Beijing–Shenzhen Highway	18.4	28 753	22 311	53.0	1.5	1.6
G108	北京－昆明公路	Beijing–Kunming Highway	80.9	3 592	2 907	29.0	0.2	0.2
G109	北京－拉萨公路	Beijing–Lhasa Highway	96.9	4 193	3 641	40.0	0.3	0.3
G110	北京－青铜峡公路	Beijing–Qingtongxia Highway	42.3	17 028	9 845	72.0	1.1	1.0
G111	北京－漠河公路	Beijing–Mohe Highway	83.0	11 564	9 574	96.0	0.8	0.6
G234	兴隆－阳江公路	Xinglong–Yangjiang Highway	251.9	4 372	3 458	108.0	0.4	0.6
G230	通化－武汉公路	Tonghua–Wuhan Highway	17.8	6 261	4 866	11.0	0.5	0.4
G335	承德－塔城公路	Chengde–Tacheng Highway	33.4	1 245	841	4.0	0.2	0.2
G509	京唐港－通州公路	Jingtang Port–Tongzhou Highway	3.9	18 684	14 416	7.0	0.6	0.6

道交通量
Highway Traffic

地点车速 (公里/时) Spot Speed (km/h)	当量 合计 Total of Equivalent	自然 合计 Total of Natural Number	汽车平均日交通量(辆/日) Average Daily Vehicle Traffic (vehicle/day)						
			小型 货车 Mini Truck	中型 货车 Medium Truck	大型 货车 Large Truck	特大 货车 Extra-large Truck	集装 箱车 Container Car	中小 客车 Mini- medium Bus	大客车 Large Bus
57.2	**11 519**	**8 719**	**653**	**604**	**295**	**515**	**76**	**6 305**	**271**
48.7	21 730	14 069	853	1 906	691	1 604	95	8 462	458
65.9	53 025	47 326	3 223	1 512	851	592	158	39 007	1 983
61.0	67 864	54 314	5 473	3 154	1 719	2 142	380	39 507	1 939
49.4	24 626	20 285	1 392	1 240	715	556	123	15 750	509
66.1	63 063	47 978	1 496	4 327	722	2 647	773	35 577	2 436
50.8	28 483	22 044	2 035	1 653	1 070	987	97	15 761	441
65.0	3 592	2 907	248	88	126	100	19	2 262	64
53.1	4 148	3 599	344	129	55	97	13	2 872	89
48.0	16 832	9 652	811	620	314	1 779	265	5 643	220
51.8	11 510	9 526	487	375	321	292	57	7 778	216
51.0	4 342	3 431	249	205	100	146	37	2 574	120
55.2	6 204	4 812	628	256	190	218	62	3 370	88
47.7	1 186	806	87	63	38	65	22	508	23
47.2	18 684	14 416	1 320	1 000	633	695	87	10 368	313

6-4 普通省
Ordinary Provincial

路线编号 Route Number	路线名称 Route Name		观测里程（公里）Observation Mileage (km)	机动车平均日交通量（辆/日）Average Daily Motor Vehicle Traffic (vehicle/day)		行驶量（万车公里/日）Vehicle Travel (10 000 vehicle-km/day)
				当量合计 Total of Equivalent	自然合计 Total of Natural Number	
	合 计	Total	892.6	16 830	12 937	1 495.0
S201	通顺路	Tongshun Road	15.9	35 832	25 349	57.0
S202	张采路	Zhangcai Road	4.7	32 294	25 093	15.0
S203	顺密路	Shunmi Road	12.7	29 718	21 126	38.0
S204	密三路	Misan Road	34.1	12 895	8 097	44.0
S205	密关路	Miguan Road	26.1	18 043	13 966	47.0
S207	觅西路	Mixi Road	1.0	16 569	14 798	2.0
S209	石担路	Shidan Road	17.1	34 332	28 840	59.0
S210	三温路	Sanwen Road	6.4	12 372	9 648	8.0
S211	斋幽路	Zhaiyou Road	25.0	912	735	2.0
S212	昌赤路	Changchi Road	28.6	3 541	3 273	10.0
S213	安四路	Ansi Road	45.7	7 923	7 359	36.0
S214	富壁路	Fubi Road	10.1	41 072	33 772	41.0
S215	京开辅路	Jingkai Side Road	7.3	22 115	17 431	16.0
S216	G6辅路	G6 Side Road	12.5	11 219	9 052	14.0
S217	康张路	Kangzhang Road	4.4	10 736	7 074	5.0
S218	温南路	Wennan Road	15.0	19 981	16 515	30.0
S219	南雁路	Nanyan Road	42.5	2 762	2 288	11.0
S220	延康路	Yankang Road	7.5	23 188	12 620	17.0
S221	孔兴路	Kongxing Road	6.1	14 459	12 440	9.0
S222	崔杏路	Cuixing Road	7.5	6 440	5 142	5.0
S223	溯小路	Huoxiao Road	11.3	4 165	3 085	5.0
S224	木燕路	Muyan Road	14.7	19 028	11 714	28.0
S225	机场东路	Airport East Road	7.5	50 267	38 979	38.0
S226	马朱路	Mazhu Road	7.4	27 150	19 056	20.0
S227	杨雁路	Yangyan Road	6.7	8 719	7 536	6.0
S228	南中轴路	Nanzhongzhou Road	17.6	12 339	8 263	22.0
S230	平程路	Pingcheng Road	10.2	6 848	5 701	7.0
S231	平兴路	Pingxing Road	8.7	3 932	3 067	3.0
S232	妫川路	Guichuan Road	6.8	19 158	14 296	13.0

道交通量
Highway Traffic

交通拥挤度 Traffic Congestion Degrees	地点车速（公里/时）Spot Speed (km/h)	汽车平均日交通量（辆/日）Average Daily Vehicle Traffic (vehicle/day)								
		当量合计 Total of Equivalent	自然合计 Total of Natural Number	小型货车 Mini Truck	中型货车 Medium Truck	大型货车 Large Truck	特大货车 Extra-large Truck	集装箱车 Container Car	中小客车 Mini-medium Bus	大客车 Large Bus
0.9	**55.1**	**16 704**	**12 814**	**1 192**	**803**	**415**	**691**	**121**	**9 147**	**445**
0.8	57.8	35 832	25 349	3 184	1 597	1 370	1 919	294	16 373	612
1.1	47.3	32 293	25 092	2 242	2 062	576	1 105	314	17 270	1 523
1.0	45.4	29 718	21 126	1 891	1 815	684	1 540	396	13 783	1 017
0.6	47.2	12 895	8 097	658	596	514	987	140	5 020	182
1.7	80.5	18 043	13 966	1 145	793	421	671	229	10 430	277
1.1	61.6	16 276	14 514	917	1 394	160	217	6	11 668	152
1.3	55.5	34 332	28 840	2 654	1 416	384	1 073	87	22 153	1 073
0.8	61.5	12 372	9 648	633	481	190	574	67	7 342	361
0.1	34.5	912	735	57	27	12	46	0	590	3
0.4	42.6	3 525	3 257	169	102	50	18	4	2 812	102
0.4	58.9	6 550	5 995	313	126	50	93	9	5 232	172
0.7	47.9	41 072	33 772	4 433	2 921	688	1 193	145	23 493	899
1.5	47.1	22 115	17 431	5 801	623	728	813	95	8 986	385
1.0	43.8	10 923	8 762	329	885	251	284	83	6 698	232
0.7	50.1	10 736	7 074	762	124	745	678	16	4 692	57
1.3	41.9	19 500	16 067	1 166	1 108	695	380	18	12 109	591
0.2	42.1	2 751	2 277	229	152	74	62	8	1 671	81
1.5	32.1	23 188	12 620	435	2 325	382	2 442	365	6 229	442
1.0	48.6	14 458	12 439	1 348	907	179	203	124	9 224	454
0.4	53.4	6 440	5 142	415	253	112	262	33	3 941	126
0.3	38.8	4 165	3 085	135	222	117	184	30	2 211	186
1.3	60.2	19 028	11 714	644	806	447	1 601	377	7 673	166
0.9	56.1	50 267	38 979	3 608	2 873	1 041	1 877	483	27 717	1 380
1.8	57.7	27 150	19 056	1 291	1 906	817	1 365	396	12 833	448
0.6	56.7	8 719	7 536	541	285	117	177	84	6 285	47
0.6	41.2	12 339	8 263	450	742	648	636	88	5 225	474
0.6	41.8	6 848	5 701	272	231	82	244	40	4 801	31
0.3	64.2	3 932	3 067	231	125	128	104	50	2 259	170
1.3	42.7	19 158	14 296	2 649	1 131	376	991	118	8 595	436

6-4

路线编号 Route Number	路线名称	Route Name	观测里程（公里）Observation Mileage (km)	机动车平均日交通量（辆/日）Average Daily Motor Vehicle Traffic (vehicle/day)		行驶量（万车公里/日）Vehicle Travel (10 000 vehicle-km/day)
				当量合计 Total of Equivalent	自然合计 Total of Natural Number	
S233	怀雁路	Huaiyan Road	5.7	22 632	21 101	13.0
S234	德贤路	Dexian Road	4.6	155 320	131 645	72.0
S302	通马路	Tongma Road	4.3	26 511	18 324	11.0
S305	顺平路	Shunping Road	24.5	27 328	21 582	67.0
S306	武兴路	Wuxing Road	7.2	17 498	15 295	12.0
S307	刘田路	Liutian Road	9.6	15 518	9 035	15.0
S308	怀长路	Huaichang Road	46.5	6 815	6 376	32.0
S309	滦赤路	Luanchi Road	11.6	1 582	1 166	2.0
S311	密兴路	Mixing Road	6.4	5 961	4 537	4.0
S312	松曹路	Songcao Road	38.6	2 732	1 799	10.0
S313	岳琉路	Yueliu Road	13.5	8 950	6 677	12.0
S314	平蓟路	Pingji Road	12.5	11 007	8 686	14.0
S315	京良路	Jingliang Road	6.5	16 817	14 570	11.0
S316	黄良路	Huangliang Road	14.6	15 440	11 411	22.0
S317	京周路	Jingzhou Road	26.7	55 857	44 637	149.0
S319	良坨路	Liangtuo Road	10.9	12 808	10 355	14.0
S320	G108复线	G108	9.4	1 958	1 814	2.0
S321	顺沙路	Shunsha Road	26.4	21 992	17 784	58.0
S322	黄马路	Huangma Road	8.3	36 220	28 991	30.0
S324	沙阳路	Shayang Road	1.5	25 475	22 226	4.0
S325	八达岭路	Badaling Road	7.2	12 892	9 698	9.0
S326	大件路	Dajian Road	10.8	40 401	31 306	44.0
S327	定泗路	Dingsi Road	11.5	20 397	18 369	23.0
S328	良三路	Liangsan Road	21.8	9 186	8 033	20.0
S329	黄亦路	Huangyi Road	16.2	21 312	18 636	34.0
S330	昌金路	Changjin Road	47.9	20 868	12 252	99.0
S331	顺平南线	Shunping South Line	39.4	11 183	7 679	44.0
S332	龙塘路	Longtang Road	16.2	22 021	14 165	36.0
S333	阎周路	Yanzhou Road	5.5	28 837	21 734	16.0
S335	白马路	Baima Road	5.6	22 864	19 838	13.0

(续表一)

交通拥挤度 Traffic Congestion Degrees	地点车速（公里/时）Spot Speed (km/h)	汽车平均日交通量（辆/日）Average Daily Vehicle Traffic (vehicle/day)								
		当量合计 Total of Equivalent	自然合计 Total of Natural Number	小型货车 Mini Truck	中型货车 Medium Truck	大型货车 Large Truck	特大货车 Extra-large Truck	集装箱车 Container Car	中小客车 Mini-medium Bus	大客车 Large Bus
0.4	83.4	22 447	20 916	652	277	84	322	9	19 109	463
2.8	76.1	155 320	131 645	9 784	8 763	3 495	2 903	42	99 721	6 937
1.8	41.0	26 511	18 324	1 507	1 173	408	1 878	219	12 151	988
0.8	57.9	27 328	21 582	1 499	1 469	455	945	300	16 180	734
1.2	57.6	17 497	15 294	1 284	969	192	352	57	12 224	216
1.0	49.2	15 518	9 035	1 078	1 624	898	1 088	169	3 970	208
0.6	55.2	6 420	6 020	352	128	48	40	7	5 247	198
0.1	46.2	1 564	1 148	215	72	74	59	14	688	26
0.4	50.6	5 961	4 537	217	1 479	296	–	–	2 360	185
0.4	42.0	2 732	1 799	217	172	82	185	28	1 026	89
0.3	42.4	8 950	6 677	645	330	120	502	62	4 665	353
0.7	59.1	11 007	8 686	371	371	254	379	111	6 885	315
1.1	63.0	16 817	14 570	638	495	234	281	75	11 919	928
0.6	43.9	15 440	11 411	1 002	1 013	436	739	92	7 813	316
1.9	56.6	55 857	44 637	6 709	2 309	1 865	1 335	492	30 218	1 709
0.8	50.4	12 808	10 355	763	315	268	480	79	8 284	166
0.3	63.8	1 600	1 456	138	54	24	20	1	1 206	13
1.0	54.9	21 921	17 749	2 606	1 171	487	677	118	12 234	456
0.8	57.5	36 220	28 991	3 863	1 468	1 543	830	121	20 054	1 112
0.5	35.6	25 425	22 176	872	1 144	220	548	122	18 816	454
1.4	51.1	12 892	9 698	497	581	171	470	196	6 656	1 127
1.3	61.9	40 401	31 306	3 184	955	1 207	1 676	300	23 432	552
1.4	40.7	19 249	17 221	1 435	1 817	351	67	1	13 122	428
0.6	45.7	9 186	8 033	217	299	130	211	8	6 995	173
1.4	52.4	21 312	18 636	1 041	857	457	211	25	14 794	1 251
1.4	47.2	20 868	12 252	688	784	419	2 203	155	7 378	625
0.7	47.5	11 183	7 679	744	643	327	641	171	4 968	185
1.5	50.3	22 021	14 165	750	825	763	1 532	357	9 436	502
1.9	63.0	28 681	21 578	1 883	1 240	1 023	1 454	0	15 827	151
0.4	57.6	22 864	19 838	2 219	941	391	377	94	15 094	722

主要统计指标解释

调查管理机构数量：指报告期末，辖区内所有公路交通量调查管理机构的数量。计量单位：个。

统计分组：按调查管理机构行政级别分为：省级、地（市）级、县乡级调查管理机构数量。

调查站点数量：指报告期末，辖区内所有交通量调查站点的数量。计量单位：个。

统计分组：一般按调查站点所在公路行政等级及调查站点设置目的进行分组。按设置目的分为：连续式调查站点、间歇式调查站点、比重调查站、车速调查路段。其中"连续式""间歇式"调查站点是指为进行交通量观测而设置的调查站，"比重调查站"是指为进行公路比重调查而设置的调查站，"车速调查路段"是指进行行程车速调查的路段。

观测里程：指调查站点所在的路段区间，也称代表路段长度。计量单位：公里。

平均日交通量：指平均每日通过公路某一断面的实际车辆数。计量单位：辆/日。

计算方法：观测记录一定时间内通过公路某一断面各种类型车辆的数量。"平均日交通量"为观测期间的交通量总数除以观测天数；"月平均日交通量"为月交通量总数除以当月的天数；"年平均日交通量"为全年交通量总数除以全年总天数。

折算交通量：指在单位时间内通过公路某一断面的折算车辆数，即折算成标准当量小客车的交通量。计量单位：辆/日。

计算方法：每类车辆的交通量与该类车辆的折算系数乘积之和。

公路交通情况调查机动车型折算系数参考值

车型	汽车							摩托车	拖拉机
一级分类	小型车		中型车		大型车	特大型车		摩托车	拖拉机
二级分类	中小客车	小型货车	大客车	中型货车	大型货车	特大型车	集装箱车		
参考折算系数	1	1	1.5	1.5	3	4	4	1	4

Explanatory Notes on Main Statistical Indicators

Number of survey management organizations refers to the number of all highway traffic survey management organizations within the jurisdiction at the end of a report. Unit:unit.

Statistical grouping: According to the administrative level of the survey management organization, it is divided into: provincial level, local (city) level, county and township level.

Number of survey stations refers to the number of all traffic survey stations within the jurisdiction at the end of the report. Unit:unit.

Statistical grouping: General by the highway administration grade and setting purposes of survey site. According to the purpose of setting, it can be divided into continuous survey station, intermittent survey station, specific gravity survey station and speed survey section. Among them, "continuous" and "intermittent" survey stations refer to the survey stations set up for traffic volume observation, ""specific gravity survey stations" refer to the survey stations set up for highway proportion survey, and "speed survey section" refers to the section for road travel speed survey.

Observation mileage refers to the section where the survey site is located, also called the length of example section. Unit: km.

Average daily traffic volume refers to the average number of actual vehicles passing through a section of the highway every day. Unit: vehicle/day.

Calculation method: Observe and record the number of various types of vehicles passing through the section of the highway in a certain period of time. "Average daily traffic volume" is the number of the total traffic volume during observation period divided by the number of days observed; "Monthly average daily traffic volume" is the number of total traffic volume of one month divided by the days in the month; "Annual average daily traffic volume" is the number of total traffic volume of one year divided by the total number of days in the year.

Converted traffic volume refers to the number of converted vehicles passing a section of the highway per unit time, which is converted into the traffic volume of standard equivalent passenger cars. Unit: vehicle/day.

Calculation method: The sum of the traffic volume for each type of vehicle multiplied by the commutative coefficient of this type of vehicle.

Highway Traffic Survey Reference Value of Conversion Coefficient of Motor Vehicle Type

Vehicle type	Vehicle							Motorcycle	Tractor
Classification I	Mini Vehicle		Medium Vehicle		Large Vehicle	Extra-large Vehicle		Motorcycle	Tractor
Classification II	Mini-medium Bus	Mini Truck	Large Bus	Medium Truck	Large Truck	Extra-large Truck	Container Car		
Reference Conversion Coefficient	1	1	1.5	1.5	3	4	4	1	4

七、附 录
APPENDIX

7-1 北京、天津、河北、上海公路基本情况
Highway of Beijing&Tianjin&Hebei&Shanghai

指标 Indicator	计量单位 Unit	北京 Beijing	天津 Tianjin	河北 Hebei	上海 Shanghai
公路里程全国排名 Highway Length National Ranking	位次 number-time	29	30	11	31
高速公路里程全国排名 Expressway Length National Ranking	位次 number-time	28	27	2	30
公路密度（以国土面积计算）Highway Density (by Territorial Area)	公里/百平方公里 km/100 sq. kms	135.62	136.61	102.96	206.69
公路里程 Length of Highway	公里 km	22 256	16 257	193 252	13 106
按行政等级分 By Administrative Level	-	-	-	-	-
国道 National Highway	公里 km	1 921	1 487	15 687	716
其中：国家高速公路 of which: National Expressway	公里 km	683	547	5 365	477
省道 Provincial Highway	公里 km	2 025	2 436	10 848	1 076
县道 County Highway	公里 km	3 856	1 296	12 002	3 101
乡道 Township Highway	公里 km	7 537	3 669	45 716	6 778
专用公路 Special Highway	公里 km	1 350	985	1 790	-
村道 Village Highway	公里 km	5 568	6 384	107 209	1 435
按技术等级分 By Technical Level	-	-	-	-	-
高速公路 Expressway	公里 km	1 115	1 262	7 280	836
一级公路 Class I Highway	公里 km	1 457	1 209	6 341	545
二级公路 Class II Highway	公里 km	4 029	2 986	20 987	3 615
三级公路 Class III Highway	公里 km	3 970	1 190	20 455	2 628
四级公路 Class IV Highway	公里 km	11 685	9 610	133 413	5 483
等外公路 Substandard Highway	公里 km	-	-	4 777	-
按路面材料分 By Pavement materials	-	-	-	-	-
沥青混凝土路面 Asphalt Concrete Pavement	公里 km	17 452	12 224	64 098	6 929
水泥混凝土路面 Cement Concrete Pavement	公里 km	4 804	4 033	104 802	6 177
简易铺装路面 Simple Pavement	公里 km	-	-	8 529	-
未铺装路面 Unpaved	公里 km	-	-	15 824	-
公路桥梁座数 Number of Highway Bridges	座 bridge	6 677	2 955	43 533	11 291
公路隧道处数 Number of Highway Tunnels	处 tunnel	135	5	727	2

7-2 全国公路里程(按行政等级分)
Length of Nationwide Highway (By Administrative Level)

单位:公里 Unit:km

地区 Region	总计 Total	国道 National Highway	国高 National Expressway	省道 Provincial Highway	县道 County Highway	乡道 Township Highway	专用公路 Special Highway	村道 Village Highway
全国总计 National Total	4 846 532	362 979	105 514	372 214	549 678	1 173 813	71 669	2 316 179
北京 Beijing	22 256	1 921	683	2 025	3 856	7 537	1 350	5 568
天津 Tianjin	16 257	1 487	547	2 436	1 296	3 669	985	6 384
河北 Hebei	193 252	15 687	5 365	10 848	12 002	45 716	1 790	107 209
山西 Shanxi	143 326	11 343	3 456	6 794	19 887	48 561	445	56 296
内蒙古 Inner Mongolia	202 641	22 264	5 607	17 489	39 395	40 108	937	82 448
辽宁 Liaoning	122 974	10 670	3 561	10 456	8 704	30 161	813	62 170
吉林 Jilin	105 399	9 860	2 654	4 893	10 711	28 310	1 577	50 048
黑龙江 Heilongjiang	167 116	14 749	3 382	13 149	3 327	49 893	18 756	67 242
上海 Shanghai	13 106	716	477	1 076	3 101	6 778	–	1 435
江苏 Jiangsu	158 729	8 323	3 449	8 540	25 343	51 956	57	64 510
浙江 Zhejiang	120 662	7 660	3 262	4 678	29 022	19 664	601	59 037
安徽 Anhui	208 826	11 006	3 632	16 526	13 546	34 438	576	132 734
福建 Fujian	108 901	10 727	3 642	5 427	15 124	41 905	123	35 596
江西 Jiangxi	161 941	11 871	4 177	12 657	21 806	41 663	16	73 928
山东 Shandong	275 642	12 892	4 575	12 814	28 142	38 101	2 166	181 525
河南 Henan	268 589	13 956	4 242	23 414	27 352	59 082	–	144 786
湖北 Hubei	275 039	14 130	4 851	19 495	27 421	83 884	611	129 498
湖南 Hunan	240 060	13 690	4 906	24 220	36 014	56 852	1 025	108 258
广东 Guangdong	217 699	15 244	6 045	21 876	9 123	99 685	135	71 636
广西 Guangxi	125 449	14 962	4 076	10 237	18 096	28 203	294	53 657
海南 Hainan	35 023	2 288	908	1 519	2 851	6 526	25	21 813
重庆 Chongqing	157 483	8 061	2 636	10 160	7 053	13 086	351	118 773
四川 Sichuan	331 592	22 462	5 031	23 405	22 695	50 036	4 799	208 195
贵州 Guizhou	196 908	11 910	3 458	20 877	34 648	45 898	–	83 575
云南 Yunnan	252 929	19 408	4 252	24 107	51 397	106 918	3 300	47 799
西藏 Tibet	97 785	13 943	38	14 978	18 346	11 759	10 332	28 426
陕西 Shaanxi	177 128	13 471	4 541	4 248	16 002	23 744	2 177	117 486
甘肃 Gansu	143 228	12 997	3 548	17 077	7 956	10 301	2 654	92 243
青海 Qinghai	82 137	13 194	3 112	8 561	9 149	21 884	1 543	27 808
宁夏 Ningxia	35 405	3 772	1 350	2 876	794	9 182	1 661	17 121
新疆 Xinjiang	189 050	18 315	4 055	15 354	25 520	58 313	12 571	58 977

7-3 全国公路里程（按技术等级分）
Length of Nationwide Highway (By Technical Level)

单位：公里　Unit:km

地区 Region		总计 Total	等级公路 Standard Highway						等外公路 Substandard Highway
			合计 Total	高速 Expressway	一级 Class I	二级 Class II	三级 Class III	四级 Class IV	
全国总计	National Total	4 846 532	4 465 864	142 593	111 703	393 471	437 060	3 381 036	380 667
北　京	Beijing	22 256	22 256	1 115	1 457	4 029	3 970	11 685	-
天　津	Tianjin	16 257	16 257	1 262	1 209	2 986	1 190	9 610	-
河　北	Hebei	193 252	188 475	7 280	6 341	20 987	20 455	133 413	4 777
山　西	Shanxi	143 326	141 012	5 605	2 731	15 736	19 422	97 518	2 314
内蒙古	Inner Mongolia	202 641	195 636	6 633	7 791	17 684	30 877	132 651	7 005
辽　宁	Liaoning	122 974	115 699	4 331	4 153	18 305	31 312	57 598	7 275
吉　林	Jilin	105 399	100 599	3 298	2 163	9 642	9 165	76 330	4 799
黑龙江	Heilongjiang	167 116	142 959	4 512	2 729	11 931	34 345	89 443	24 156
上　海	Shanghai	13 106	13 106	836	545	3 615	2 628	5 483	-
江　苏	Jiangsu	158 729	156 297	4 711	15 081	23 439	16 261	96 805	2 432
浙　江	Zhejiang	120 662	120 339	4 421	7 046	10 374	8 860	89 638	323
安　徽	Anhui	208 826	207 942	4 836	4 863	11 595	19 939	166 708	885
福　建	Fujian	108 901	92 464	5 155	1 351	10 887	8 502	66 568	16 438
江　西	Jiangxi	161 941	135 442	5 931	2 601	11 613	14 338	100 959	26 499
山　东	Shandong	275 642	274 948	6 057	11 159	26 177	29 443	202 112	693
河　南	Henan	268 589	242 775	6 600	3 692	27 192	21 470	183 822	25 814
湖　北	Hubei	275 039	265 912	6 367	6 093	23 179	11 035	219 237	9 128
湖　南	Hunan	240 060	223 667	6 725	2 068	14 478	5 798	194 599	16 393
广　东	Guangdong	217 699	209 131	9 003	11 329	18 975	19 185	150 640	8 568
广　西	Guangxi	125 449	115 702	5 563	1 554	13 156	8 676	86 753	9 748
海　南	Hainan	35 023	34 731	924	460	1 845	1 615	29 886	292
重　庆	Chongqing	157 483	133 943	3 096	952	8 572	5 717	115 605	23 541
四　川	Sichuan	331 592	304 830	7 131	4 178	16 021	14 636	262 864	26 762
贵　州	Guizhou	196 908	156 559	6 453	1 464	8 433	6 918	133 291	40 348
云　南	Yunnan	252 929	220 554	5 184	1 443	12 222	9 715	191 991	32 374
西　藏	Tibet	97 785	85 473	38	578	1 055	10 818	72 984	12 312
陕　西	Shaanxi	177 128	161 028	5 475	1 641	9 734	15 891	128 288	16 100
甘　肃	Gansu	143 228	128 071	4 242	627	9 156	13 707	100 338	15 157
青　海	Qinghai	82 137	70 157	3 328	609	8 525	5 001	52 694	11 980
宁　夏	Ningxia	35 405	35 355	1 678	1 895	3 870	6 205	21 706	51
新　疆	Xinjiang	189 050	154 546	4 803	1 901	18 056	29 968	99 817	34 504

7-4 全国高速公路里程
Length of Nationwide Expressway

单位：公里　Unit:km

地区 Region		高速公路 Expressway				车道里程 Length of Lane
		合计 Total	四车道 4-lane	六车道 6-lane	八车道及以上 8-lane and above	
全国总计	National Total	142 593	116 997	19 757	5 840	633 310
北 京	Beijing	1 115	507	539	68	5 810
天 津	Tianjin	1 262	358	769	135	7 126
河 北	Hebei	7 280	4 818	1 956	506	35 056
山 西	Shanxi	5 605	4 649	943	13	24 357
内蒙古	Inner Mongolia	6 633	6 135	273	224	27 975
辽 宁	Liaoning	4 331	3 345	337	650	20 599
吉 林	Jilin	3 298	3 139	62	98	13 708
黑龙江	Heilongjiang	4 512	4 512	–	–	18 047
上 海	Shanghai	836	245	389	201	4 924
江 苏	Jiangsu	4 711	2 604	1 750	357	23 773
浙 江	Zhejiang	4 421	2 992	884	544	21 631
安 徽	Anhui	4 836	4 429	346	61	20 294
福 建	Fujian	5 155	4 012	801	342	23 593
江 西	Jiangxi	5 931	5 593	236	103	24 608
山 东	Shandong	6 057	5 082	940	35	26 249
河 南	Henan	6 600	5 011	562	1 027	31 631
湖 北	Hubei	6 367	5 967	345	55	26 377
湖 南	Hunan	6 725	6 299	425	–	27 749
广 东	Guangdong	9 003	4 473	4 000	529	46 181
广 西	Guangxi	5 563	5 127	115	321	23 768
海 南	Hainan	924	892	33	–	3 762
重 庆	Chongqing	3 096	2 637	459	–	13 303
四 川	Sichuan	7 131	6 331	783	17	30 160
贵 州	Guizhou	6 453	6 116	338	–	26 488
云 南	Yunnan	5 184	3 930	1 165	89	23 420
西 藏	Tibet	38	38	–	–	151
陕 西	Shaanxi	5 475	4 110	1 031	335	25 298
甘 肃	Gansu	4 242	4 133	85	24	17 234
青 海	Qinghai	3 328	3 256	72	–	13 456
宁 夏	Ningxia	1 678	1 559	15	105	7 162
新 疆	Xinjiang	4 803	4 699	104	–	19 421

7-5 全国公路密度及通达率
Density and Service Rate of Nationwide Highway

地区 Region	公路密度 Highway Density	
	以国土面积计算（公里/百平方公里） By Territorial Area (km/100 sq. km)	以人口计算（公里/万人） By Population (km/10 000 persons)
全国总计 National Total	**50.48**	**34.73**
北京 Beijing	135.62	11.03
天津 Tianjin	136.61	10.44
河北 Hebei	102.96	25.70
山西 Shanxi	91.70	38.93
内蒙古 Inner Mongolia	17.13	80.14
辽宁 Liaoning	84.29	29.30
吉林 Jilin	56.24	38.79
黑龙江 Heilongjiang	36.81	43.59
上海 Shanghai	206.69	5.42
江苏 Jiangsu	154.71	19.44
浙江 Zhejiang	118.53	24.34
安徽 Anhui	149.48	29.58
福建 Fujian	89.70	27.84
江西 Jiangxi	97.03	35.14
山东 Shandong	175.90	28.75
河南 Henan	160.83	28.02
湖北 Hubei	147.95	46.60
湖南 Hunan	113.34	36.21
广东 Guangdong	122.37	19.49
广西 Guangxi	53.00	22.40
海南 Hainan	103.31	37.83
重庆 Chongqing	191.12	51.20
四川 Sichuan	68.00	36.29
贵州 Guizhou	111.82	55.00
云南 Yunnan	64.20	52.69
西藏 Tibet	7.96	290.03
陕西 Shaanxi	86.15	46.94
甘肃 Gansu	31.52	51.83
青海 Qinghai	11.39	140.48
宁夏 Ningxia	53.32	52.46
新疆 Xinjiang	11.39	78.84

7-6 全国公路客、货运输量
Passenger and Freight Traffic of Nationwide Highway

地区 Region	客运量（万人） Passenger Traffic (10 000 persons)	旅客周转量（万人公里） Turnover of Passenger Traffic (10 000 person-kms)	货运量（万吨） Freight Traffic (10 000 tons)	货物周转量（万吨公里） Turnover of Freight Traffic (10 000 ton-kms)
全国总计 National Total	1 367 170	92 796 786	3 956 871	712 492 119
北京 Beijing	44 577	998 670	20 278	1 674 068
天津 Tianjin	12 259	763 991	34 711	4 041 043
河北 Hebei	35 133	2 276 120	226 334	85 501 489
山西 Shanxi	15 719	1 596 433	126 214	19 077 478
内蒙古 Inner Mongolia	7 823	1 224 299	160 018	29 856 260
辽宁 Liaoning	56 355	2 914 584	189 737	31 522 946
吉林 Jilin	23 372	1 537 688	46 520	11 892 270
黑龙江 Heilongjiang	20 739	1 541 311	42 943	8 106 627
上海 Shanghai	3 151	1 058 150	39 595	2 992 852
江苏 Jiangsu	97 025	7 166 416	139 251	25 443 508
浙江 Zhejiang	72 013	4 027 998	166 533	19 640 996
安徽 Anhui	50 770	3 768 861	283 817	54 516 155
福建 Fujian	34 081	2 120 353	96 576	12 895 222
江西 Jiangxi	49 302	2 609 677	157 646	37 599 405
山东 Shandong	50 044	4 935 669	312 807	68 596 754
河南 Henan	93 707	7 111 879	235 183	58 939 218
湖北 Hubei	80 990	4 534 386	163 145	29 555 342
湖南 Hunan	91 007	4 799 324	204 389	31 148 474
广东 Guangdong	105 249	11 207 070	304 743	38 903 239
广西 Guangxi	36 134	3 510 955	153 389	26 830 499
海南 Hainan	9 637	743 811	12 052	845 547
重庆 Chongqing	52 150	2 604 300	107 064	11 527 546
四川 Sichuan	81 462	4 661 427	173 324	18 149 501
贵州 Guizhou	84 053	4 690 756	95 354	11 465 112
云南 Yunnan	34 642	2 696 330	135 321	14 892 305
西藏 Tibet	1 047	279 658	2 363	1 168 409
陕西 Shaanxi	60 269	2 869 830	130 823	23 013 743
甘肃 Gansu	36 634	2 333 051	64 271	11 189 739
青海 Qinghai	5 092	507 669	15 685	2 757 436
宁夏 Ningxia	5 342	474 610	31 757	3 981 942
新疆 Xinjiang	17 394	1 231 513	85 029	14 766 994

7-7 全国城市客运设施
National Urban Passenger Transport Facilities

地区 Region	公交专用车道长度（公里） Length of Bus Lanes (km)	轨道交通车站数（个） Rail Transit Station(unit)	换乘站数 Number of Transfer Station
全国总计 National Total	12 850.2	3 408	319
北 京 Beijing	952.0	391	59
天 津 Tianjin	65.0	152	16
河 北 Hebei	304.8	25	1
山 西 Shanxi	495.2	-	-
内蒙古 Inner Mongolia	330.3	-	-
辽 宁 Liaoning	1 028.0	150	4
吉 林 Jilin	242.3	129	4
黑龙江 Heilongjiang	117.0	22	1
上 海 Shanghai	363.7	415	60
江 苏 Jiangsu	1 228.4	392	22
浙 江 Zhejiang	906.1	131	16
安 徽 Anhui	302.1	46	1
福 建 Fujian	246.2	45	-
江 西 Jiangxi	131.4	40	1
山 东 Shandong	1 145.0	91	3
河 南 Henan	786.1	60	1
湖 北 Hubei	438.2	206	23
湖 南 Hunan	496.4	46	2
广 东 Guangdong	1 449.7	491	61
广 西 Guangxi	268.8	41	2
海 南 Hainan	25.0	-	-
重 庆 Chongqing	121.9	179	19
四 川 Sichuan	635.2	168	14
贵 州 Guizhou	95.0	24	-
云 南 Yunnan	94.4	57	3
西 藏 Tibet	-	-	-
陕 西 Shaanxi	269.6	95	6
甘 肃 Gansu	15.4	-	-
青 海 Qinghai	15.0	-	-
宁 夏 Ningxia	132.0	-	-
新 疆 Xinjiang	150.0	12	-

注：上海轨道交通车站数含江苏（昆山）境内3个，换乘站数0个。
Note: The number of Shanghai rail transit stations includes 3 stations and 0 transfer station in Jiangsu (Kunshan).

7-8 全国公共汽电车客运量
National Public Trolley Buses Traffic Volume

地区	Region	运营里程（万公里）Operating Length (10 000 kms)	客运量（万人次）Passenger Traffic (10 000 person-times)	BRT
全国总计	National Total	3 460 969	6 969 986	158 652
北　京	Beijing	126 880	318 976	4 760
天　津	Tianjin	47 304	109 725	—
河　北	Hebei	127 984	197 574	—
山　西	Shanxi	66 024	160 180	—
内蒙古	Inner Mongolia	64 294	116 198	264
辽　宁	Liaoning	132 123	382 255	1 593
吉　林	Jilin	66 400	163 430	—
黑龙江	Heilongjiang	106 336	245 878	—
上　海	Shanghai	103 844	206 233	—
江　苏	Jiangsu	252 972	460 823	19 176
浙　江	Zhejiang	229 468	380 460	11 222
安　徽	Anhui	114 814	204 020	11 929
福　建	Fujian	108 396	216 581	9 801
江　西	Jiangxi	77 157	128 513	—
山　东	Shandong	261 270	382 230	7 320
河　南	Henan	146 143	273 180	31 494
湖　北	Hubei	145 260	330 055	4 341
湖　南	Hunan	142 468	286 632	1 173
广　东	Guangdong	421 132	616 970	21 658
广　西	Guangxi	73 315	117 922	3 813
海　南	Hainan	27 057	33 221	—
重　庆	Chongqing	78 964	252 715	—
四　川	Sichuan	156 949	400 746	9 045
贵　州	Guizhou	56 862	187 797	3 038
云　南	Yunnan	84 308	164 757	—
西　藏	Tibet	3 884	9 628	—
陕　西	Shaanxi	91 189	243 630	—
甘　肃	Gansu	51 416	146 587	3 930
青　海	Qinghai	20 996	45 448	—
宁　夏	Ningxia	18 440	40 041	1 397
新　疆	Xinjiang	57 320	147 584	12 698

7-9 全国轨道交通运量
National Rail Transit Traffic Volume

地区 Region	运营车公里 （万车公里） Operation Vehicle Kilometrage (10 000 vehicle-kms)	客运量 （万人次） Passenger Traffic (10 000 person-times)	旅客周转量 （万人公里） Turnover of Passenger Traffic (10 000 person-kms)
全国总计 National Total	352 602	2 127 659	17 952 115
北京 Beijing	59 861	384 842	3 357 615
天津 Tianjin	9 985	40 834	513 464
河北 Hebei	1 484	8 760	50 651
山西 Shanxi	—	—	—
内蒙古 Inner Mongolia	—	—	—
辽宁 Liaoning	9 846	52 642	454 776
吉林 Jilin	2 647	14 200	87 200
黑龙江 Heilongjiang	1 380	8 269	57 029
上海 Shanghai	56 242	370 592	3 374 896
江苏 Jiangsu	33 519	155 924	1 242 036
浙江 Zhejiang	15 371	65 422	561 903
安徽 Anhui	3 723	15 324	116 350
福建 Fujian	3 215	10 252	86 574
江西 Jiangxi	3 033	14 176	103 967
山东 Shandong	4 810	15 388	124 411
河南 Henan	6 274	29 341	271 786
湖北 Hubei	18 436	103 710	795 666
湖南 Hunan	4 284	25 030	185 560
广东 Guangdong	64 096	495 175	3 929 575
广西 Guangxi	3 534	21 361	159 509
海南 Hainan	—	—	—
重庆 Chongqing	17 868	85 787	798 894
四川 Sichuan	17 190	115 756	900 746
贵州 Guizhou	742	744	5 903
云南 Yunnan	4 798	19 958	196 505
西藏 Tibet	—	—	—
陕西 Shaanxi	10 146	73 930	575 324
甘肃 Gansu	—	—	—
青海 Qinghai	—	—	—
宁夏 Ningxia	—	—	—
新疆 Xinjiang	119	244	1 778

注：上海轨道交通客运量含江苏（昆山）境内约 2 149 万人次。
Note: Passenger traffic of Shanghai rail transit includes about 21.49 million passenger-times in Jiangsu (kunshan).

7-10 全国出租汽车运量
National Taxi Traffic Volume

地区 Region	载客车次总数（万车次）Total Number of Passenger Trips (10 000 vehicle-times)	运营里程（万公里）Operating Length (10 000 kms)	载客里程 Passenger Transportation Length	客运量（万人次）Passenger Traffic (10 000 person-times)
全国总计 National Total	1 859 107	15 068 478	9 981 177	3 516 674
北京 Beijing	24 301	438 870	281 000	34 021
天津 Tianjin	20 615	328 364	177 311	36 860
河北 Hebei	72 112	757 434	503 385	133 444
山西 Shanxi	53 698	407 282	264 654	105 949
内蒙古 Inner Mongolia	87 225	637 201	419 504	158 028
辽宁 Liaoning	136 905	1 149 076	781 780	265 450
吉林 Jilin	93 725	752 426	570 406	185 033
黑龙江 Heilongjiang	156 971	940 162	647 194	316 783
上海 Shanghai	35 422	511 778	317 853	63 760
江苏 Jiangsu	60 164	607 512	345 801	124 851
浙江 Zhejiang	57 163	523 841	312 726	103 745
安徽 Anhui	85 272	627 493	422 118	167 332
福建 Fujian	29 944	257 256	167 865	57 726
江西 Jiangxi	28 213	189 358	113 706	55 848
山东 Shandong	73 766	768 726	489 617	125 717
河南 Henan	81 953	686 445	474 193	148 545
湖北 Hubei	72 986	622 440	392 431	138 151
湖南 Hunan	76 274	449 714	302 484	155 044
广东 Guangdong	77 272	801 293	507 693	144 143
广西 Guangxi	25 574	255 033	159 926	34 023
海南 Hainan	7 239	97 283	62 977	16 093
重庆 Chongqing	54 296	398 201	264 470	112 454
四川 Sichuan	89 610	585 263	379 773	171 972
贵州 Guizhou	65 554	309 782	235 460	141 056
云南 Yunnan	42 587	236 795	155 434	82 956
西藏 Tibet	6 994	48 075	37 218	12 618
陕西 Shaanxi	66 144	466 857	316 572	123 179
甘肃 Gansu	48 181	357 597	256 348	85 605
青海 Qinghai	18 217	131 779	105 673	31 332
宁夏 Ningxia	21 431	147 044	99 800	38 181
新疆 Xinjiang	89 301	578 100	415 804	146 776